Brazil

Polity Histories series

Jeff Kingston, *Japan*
David W. Lesch, *Syria*
Dmitri Trenin, *Russia*
Kerry Brown, *China*
Emile Chabal, *France*
Alan Dowty, *Israel*
Adrian Bingham, *United Kingdom*

Brazil

Joel Wolfe

polity

Copyright © Joel Wolfe 2023

The right of Joel Wolfe to be identified as Author of this Work has been asserted in accordance with the UK Copyright, Designs and Patents Act 1988.

First published in 2023 by Polity Press

Polity Press
65 Bridge Street
Cambridge CB2 1UR, UK

Polity Press
111 River Street
Hoboken, NJ 07030, USA

All rights reserved. Except for the quotation of short passages for the purpose of criticism and review, no part of this publication may be reproduced, stored in a retrieval system or transmitted, in any form or by any means, electronic, mechanical, photocopying, recording or otherwise, without the prior permission of the publisher.

ISBN-13: 978-1-5095-4775-3
ISBN-13: 978-1-5095-4776-0 (pb)

A catalogue record for this book is available from the British Library.

Library of Congress Control Number: 2022950420

Typeset in 11 on 13 Berkeley by
Cheshire Typesetting Ltd, Cuddington, Cheshire
Printed and bound in the UK by TJ International Ltd

The publisher has used its best endeavours to ensure that the URLs for external websites referred to in this book are correct and active at the time of going to press. However, the publisher has no responsibility for the websites and can make no guarantee that a site will remain live or that the content is or will remain appropriate.

Every effort has been made to trace all copyright holders, but if any have been overlooked the publisher will be pleased to include any necessary credits in any subsequent reprint or edition.

For further information on Polity, visit our website:
politybooks.com

In memory of my friend and mentor Tom Skidmore

Contents

Map	viii
Acronyms, Abbreviations, and Glossary	ix
Acknowledgments	xiv
Introduction	1
1 Tropical Liberalism (1840–1930)	19
2 The Failed March to Modernity (1930–1964)	51
3 Military Dictatorship (1964–1985)	86
4 Chaotic Democracy (1985–1994)	115
5 The Triumph of Social Democracy (1994–2010)	141
6 The Great Unraveling (2010–)	167
Afterword	194
Further Reading	200
Index	211

Map of Brazil and its neighborhood

Acronyms, Abbreviations, and Glossary

Abertura	Opening
AEB	Agência Espacial Brasileira or Brazilian Space Agency
ARENA	Aliança Renovadora Nacional or National Renewal Alliance
BNDES	Banco Nacional de Desenvolvimento Econômico e Social or National Bank for Economic Development
Bolsa Família	Family Stipend
BRIC	Brazil, Russia, India, China
Cariocas	Residents of the city of Rio de Janeiro
Centrão	The Big Center, a collection of centrist and conservative political parties in the Congress
CNC	Conselho Nacional do Café or National Coffee Council
Colonos	Immigrant coffee workers, primarily in São Paulo
Coronéis	Rural bosses

ACRONYMS, ABBREVIATIONS, AND GLOSSARY

DIEESE	Departamento Intersindical de Estatíticas e Estudos Sócio-Econômicos or Inter-Union Department of Statistics and Socio-Economic Studies
DIP	Departamento de Imprensa e Propaganda or Department of Press and Propaganda
"Diretas Já"	"Direct Elections Now"
ECLA/CEPAL	Economic Commission for Latin America/Comisión Económica para América Latina
Electrobras	National Electric Utility Company
Estado Novo	New State Dictatorship, 1937–45
FHC	Fernando Henrique Cardoso
Fome Zero	Zero Hunger
Frente Negra	Black Front
Gaúcho	Someone or something from the state of Rio Grande do Sul
GDP	Gross domestic product
Grito de Inpiranga	Cry of Inpiranga (declaration of independence)
IHGB	Instituto Histórico e Geográfico Brasileiro or Brazilian Historical and Geographical Institute

ACRONYMS, ABBREVIATIONS, AND GLOSSARY

Imposto sindical	Union tax
Institutional Acts	Declarations of law made by military dictatorship
JK	Juscelino Kubitschek
MDB	Movimento Democrático Brasileiro or Brazilian Democratic Movement
Mensalão	Monthly Allowance, which became a system of bribes to members of Congress
Mineiro	Someone or something from the state of Minas Gerais
NAFTA	North American Free Trade Agreement
Operação Lava Jato	Operation Car Wash
Paulista	Someone or something from the state of São Paulo
Paulistano	Someone or something from the city of São Paulo
PCB	Partido Communista Brasileiro or Communist Party of Brazil (Soviet-aligned)
PC do B	Partido Communista do Brasil or Communist Party of Brazil (Maoist)
PDC	Partido Democrata Cristão or Christian Democratic Party

PDS	Partido Democrático Social or Democratic Social Party
PDT	Partido Democrático Trabalhista or Democratic Labor Party
Petrobras	National Oil Company
PFL	Partido da Frente Liberal or Liberal Democratic Front
PIN	Programa de Integração Nacional or National Integration Program
PJ	Partido de Juventude or Youth Party
PL	Partido Liberal or Liberal Party
PLS	Partido Liberal Social or Liberal Social Party
PMDB	Partido do Movimento Democrático Brasileiro or Party of the Brazilian Democratic Movement
PPS	Partido Popular Socialista or Popular Socialist Party
PRN	Partido de Reconstrução Nacional or National Reconstruction Party
Proálcool	National Ethanol Program
PRONA	Partido de Reedificação da Ordem Nacional or Party of the Reconstruction of the Nation

PSB	Partido Socialista Brasileiro or Brazilian Socialist Party
PSD	Partido Social Democrático or Social Democratic Party
PSDB	Partido da Social Democracia Brasileira or Brazilian Social Democratic Party
PSP	Partido Social Progressista or Social Progressive Party
PT	Partido dos Trabalhadores or Workers' Party
PTB	Partido Trabahista Brasileiro or Brazilian Labor Party
PTN	Partido Trabalhista Nacional or National Labor Party
Quilombos	Runaway slave communities
SALTE	*Saúde, Alimentação, Transportação, Energia* or Health, Food, Transporation, Energy
Sindicalizado/a	Formally unionized
Telebrás	National Telephone Company
Tenentes	Young, rebellious military officers
UDN	União Democrático Nacional or Democratic National Union
USP	University of São Paulo

Acknowledgments

I wrote most of this book during the Covid-19 pandemic, and so relied on Zoom calls and emails with colleagues for discussions about it. I am particularly grateful to two wonderful UMass Amherst graduate students, Yuri Gama and Jorge Minella, who were both in Brazil during much of the pandemic. Our twice-monthly Zoom meetings about their dissertations always included broader historiographical discussions, followed by analyses of the current political situation there. They both read portions of the manuscript, and I am grateful for their tough questions and terrific insights.

The book also benefited from ongoing conversations about Brazil with Roger Kittleson and Todd Diacon. My UMass colleague Steve Platt, a historian of China, has provided a great deal of encouragement and intellectual support, and I thank him for it. Inès Boxman and Louise Knight at Polity Press have been patient and thoughtful in guiding me throughout this project. I cannot thank them enough.

My family is always the most supportive of my teaching and scholarship. My wife, Traci, and I have done our jobs from home in close physical proximity over the course of the last 18 months, and we learned more about each other's work in that year and a half than we had in our previous 30 years together. I thank her for her support and good humor throughout. Work on this book began just as our son Ted was finishing his senior thesis on the 1792 yellow fever outbreak and panic in Philadelphia, and I completed it as our daughter, Ellie, began writing her senior honors thesis on women in South Africa's anti-apartheid movement. While neither aspires to become a historian, their creativity and hard work on their theses inspired me to complete this book. Ellie's frequent questions about my progress also often prodded me to get back to work, and I thank her for that.

Finally, I have dedicated this book to Tom Skidmore, my graduate advisor at the University of Wisconsin. In addition to being one of the most insightful and prolific scholars of modern Brazilian history and politics, Tom was a great teacher and friend. His intelligence, humor, and humanity first inspired me years ago in Madison, and they continue to do so today.

Introduction

In August 2022, a Brazilian Air Force jet landed in Brasília. The plane carried a high-ranking Portuguese military officer who brought a reliquary containing the embalmed heart of Pedro I, the European-born monarch who had declared Brazilian independence on September 7, 1822. President Jair Bolsonaro promoted bringing Pedro I's heart to Brazil's modernist capital (the former monarch returned to Portugal in 1831 after losing the support of the nation's powerful planter class, and died there in 1834) to be part of the nation's bicentennial celebration. The reality was that Bolsonaro celebrated the long-dead Portuguese-Brazilian sovereign for very specific, twenty-first-century reasons. The controversial president brought back the European-born emperor's heart to signal a conservative, even revanchist, political identity as the October 2022 elections loomed.

Pedro I declared independence from his father's monarchy by declaring "*Fico!*," or "I stay!" He and the slaveholding planters who backed him had no intention of changing the economy or social structure. Bolsonaro's embrace of Pedro I was far from subtle. He was associating himself with a white, conservative politics that contrasted with those of his main opponent,

Luiz Inácio Lula da Silva, who had governed Brazil from 2003 to 2010 as the leader of the social democratic Workers' Party (Partido dos Trabalhadores or PT). On September 7, 2022, Bolsonaro did not preside over a non-partisan celebration of Brazil's history, present circumstances, and hopes for the future. He held a series of campaign rallies in which he openly critiqued Lula and his record. In the days leading up to September 7, political commentators publicly worried that Bolsonaro might use the bicentennial celebrations to initiate violent actions against his opponents, especially Lula. He spoke of the day as "our last chance" to save the nation from the left. For his part, Lula described Bolsonaro's September 7 events as being more like a Ku Klux Klan rally than a national celebration of independence.

On the day of the bicentennial, the government put on displays of military might, with tanks, fighter jets, and warships in and around São Paulo, Rio de Janeiro, and Brasília. There was no reckoning with the nation's past or hopes for the future. The military displays were the only patriotic gesture. Throughout the rest of day, the president used the two hundredth anniversary of Brazilian independence as a chance to campaign for reelection on October 2. Bolsonaro did not bother to celebrate the nation's now long embrace of democracy after the 1964–85 military dictatorship. Instead, he claimed that voting machines (the very devices that were used to elect him president four years earlier) were untrustworthy and easily hacked.

In the past, he had even hinted that he might not relinquish his office if he were to lose the election.

Brazil's Foundational Myths

Beyond the crassness of hijacking the nation's bicentennial for a campaign event, Bolsonaro's embrace of Pedro I and of the military highlight Brazil's complex and incomplete history, as well as the contentiousness of its present-day politics. Brazil has long been defined by a series of superlatives, both constructive and negative. It is Latin America's largest and most populous nation. In the nineteenth century, Brazil had the largest slave population in the world. It had a peaceful transition from colony to nation, and so avoided the violence that defined the nineteenth century in much of South America and Mexico. Brazil had a long nineteenth century of macro-level political stability, but it also did not abolish slavery until 1888. It has continued to be defined by similar contradictions throughout the twentieth century around everything from the struggle over dictatorship and democracy to the ways its advanced manufacturing sector contrasts with extreme poverty in both the urban and rural sectors. And, although the twenty-first century began with much hope as Brazil's stable polity and growing economy led many at home and abroad to believe that this really was the country of tomorrow, the last decade has been so turbulent that a sitting president threatened to ignore electoral results he did not like.

These contradictions are embedded in a series of myths that have shaped how Brazilians and others see the country. The easy path to independence and the decades of political stability that lasted from 1822 to the onset of the Great Depression in 1930 have led to the Myth of Conciliation (*conciliação*). Brazilians and others tend to embrace the idea that the country is less violent than most, especially compared to its neighbors in Latin America. This glosses over the very real violence embedded in a slave society, as well as the violence that has been used throughout Brazilian history to maintain the social order. Although this myth is obviously not true, it does shape how Brazilians think and act. Likewise the Myth of Racial Democracy is simultaneously fanciful and powerful. This myth holds that there is a sort of racial social mobility in Brazil that juxtaposes a more fluid system of race with the more rigid system in the United States. This is a soothing idea for many white Brazilians and a source of pride for even more as they compare favorably the ways race shapes their nation compared to the way it does in the United States. The idea that Brazil is a racial democracy has affected the ways people talk about racism, and limited solutions to the racial inequities for at least a century after abolition. Rejection of this myth by many has also brought a backlash from the political right. The way Bolsonaro and Lula differ on the subject lays bare the stark divide.

The Myth of the Future is the final way of thinking that has long shaped Brazilian history. It is hard to know exactly when Brazilians began to discount the past. After abolition in 1888, the national government burned records related to most aspects of slavery. It was an attempt to erase some of the nation's history. During much of the twentieth and still today, Brazilian leaders have discounted the past and even the present by embracing the idea that Brazil is destined to be one of the world's leading nations. The opening of the new national capital in Brazil's interior in 1960 was an obvious expression of that. The embrace of new technologies (e.g. the automobile and airplane) and new commodity finds (especially petroleum) gave Brazilians of various generations the opportunity to imagine a modern and prosperous nation awaiting them in the near future.

Embracing these myths has allowed Brazilians to see their past and present through a warped lens. Telling themselves that they are more peaceful and so in many ways better than their Spanish American neighbors allows them to look past Brazil's very real dilemmas. Believing that there is some sort of mechanism of racial democracy means that they do not have to do the heavy lifting of addressing their country's very real legacy of racism. And a belief that your future is almost preordained to be better than your present further relieves Brazilians of undertaking the hard work of analyzing real problems and creating effective solutions for them. This has left Brazil in an ongoing state of becoming a modern nation, but without quite achieving that status. The political turmoil of the last decade, after a quarter-century of imperfect democracy, but democracy nonetheless, is another marker of the incomplete nature of Brazilian national development.

A Contested History and Incomplete State Making

The notion of a nation being incomplete is not unique to Brazil or the Global South. The United States was hardly a coherent or unified nation in the years before its Civil War (1861–5). There are also much less drastic examples of incomplete nations in the twentieth and twenty-first centuries. Some nations, such as Brazil, Canada, and Spain, have been organized in ways that encourage the ongoing power of centrifugal forces that preclude the development of a strong central state. In Canada's case, the provinces retain power that limits Ottawa's capacity to govern the nation. Spain developed a weak central state in part because it continued to focus governing capacity on its colonial possessions until the end of the nineteenth century. As this book shows, Brazil's weak central government and its incomplete nature are rooted in its colonial and national histories. In 1960, the nation's leaders inaugurated a new interior national capital city explicitly to address those very issues.

Brasília opened nearly five hundred years after the Portuguese navigator and explorer Pedro Álvarez Cabral stumbled upon Brazil in 1500. The Portuguese nobleman was leading a fleet of 14 ships to India, but he tacked to the west to avoid the poor winds in Africa's Gulf of Guinea. Cabral and his men made landfall on April 22, 1500, on what they believed to be an Atlantic island, but was in fact present-day Porto Seguro in the Brazilian state of Bahia. At that time, Portugal was the world's leading seafaring nation. The Portuguese had trading outposts (known as "forts" or "factories") along the West African coast and in Goa on the Indian mainland. The Portuguese would expand their Asian trade using Macao off the coast of Canton, China, as a base of operations. Unlike the Spanish, who sought to convert large indigenous populations to Christianity, the Portuguese really only wanted to trade. They even named their new possession Brazil after the first export they had bartered for with the local inhabitants, brazilwood. The Portuguese also did not encounter large, urban-based indigenous populations like those the Spanish conquered in Meso-America and the Andes. Brazil's indigenous people were semi-nomadic and nomadic, and so many of them easily fled Portuguese attempts to enslave or otherwise coerce them into labor. These differences between the Spanish colonial project of large-scale conversion and the transformation of indigenous cities such as Tenochtitlan into present-day Mexico City, on the one hand, and the Portuguese desire to trade and later develop commodities for export, on the other, had long-term consequences for national development in Latin America, and set Brazil on a different course from countries such as Mexico and Peru.

Throughout the colonial period (1500–1808), Portuguese policy was often reactive to the presence of other European powers and to opportunities in the world economy. Initially only visiting trading forts, the Portuguese moved south from Bahia to take French Antarctique (Rio de Janeiro) in 1567, and later solidified their hold on much of the Northeast by dislodging the Dutch in 1654, who had established colonies there beginning in 1630. Increasing European demand for sugar led the Portuguese to establish plantations in the Northeast. After failing to enslave indigenous people, who, as noted, could easily flee into the interior, they quickly began importing African slaves to work the plantations. Even as these plantations flourished, there was no clear plan or even idea of what Brazil was. The colony began on the Atlantic coast, but some officials described its dimensions as being from the coast "*até o fim do mundo*" (until the end of the world). This was no idle comment. The initial, official designation of administrative units demarcated so-called Donatary Captaincies that were measured on the coast with a sextant. They had clean latitudinal borders, but no longitudinal end.

Individuals and families controlled the Donatary Captaincies. As sugar production demonstrated the viability of the colony, and in order to more coherently fight off other Europeans' interest in the territory, the Portuguese crown established more direct control over Brazil during the second half of the sixteenth century. In doing so, Lisbon ended the Donatary Captaincies.

The style of limited centralized control had begun. There were a few port cities in the Northeast, such as Salvador and Recife, for imports and exports, but early Brazilian society revolved around plantations, especially those producing sugar. Although the colony grew, colonists were said to "hug the coast like crabs" as sugar production and trade with indigenous people made up the bulk of economic activity until gold and diamonds were discovered in the near interior of the Center-South in the present-day state of Minas Gerais (General Mines) in 1695. The mining boom that followed brought the first sustained Portuguese presence off the coast. It also forced Lisbon to move the colonial capital to Rio de Janeiro to place government officials closer to this new source of wealth in order to try to stem the rampant smuggling that had developed along with the mining industry.

Both large-scale sugar plantations and small mining operations relied almost exclusively on African slaves. The profitability of sugar and later diamond and gold mining, along with the Portuguese previous experience with African chattel slavery on Cape Verde and other sugar-producing Atlantic islands, began the process whereby Brazil would eventually become the world's largest slaveholding society. It was also the last nation in the Western Hemisphere to end slavery.

Unlike the Spanish, French, and English, the Portuguese had not at first planned to create large settlements in the Americas. However, while they were not sure what to make of these new lands, they were sure they did not want other European powers on them. They had not planned to create sugar plantations, but they did not shy away from doing so when it became feasible and then profitable. The discovery of precious metals deepened the interest of the Portuguese in their colony. But the haphazard nature of how they organized it had long-term implications for how Brazil would develop economically, socially, and politically over the more than five hundred years following Cabral's landfall.

Debating the Meaning of Brazil

Beginning in the mid-nineteenth century, Brazilian intellectuals began to write about these issues. In 1838, a group of political leaders, many of whom had been born and educated in Portugal, founded the Brazilian Historical and Geographical Institute (Instituto Histórico e Geográfico Brasileiro or IHGB) to study the land and its people. By the 1850s, the IHGB had been taken over by Brazilian-born and -educated scholars who began to analyze more critically their nation. Brazil's first great national historian, João de Capistrano de Abreu (1853–1927), expanded on this work with a series of books that detailed the nation's colonial roots, with a particular focus on what he termed "the peopling of Brazil." Capistrano de Abreu was fascinated by the ways Europeans and others moved throughout the land in search of new economic and social possibilities. Later scholars took that idea even further in that the slave catchers who hunted down runaways in the interior were transformed into honorable frontiersmen. No matter what their political or social perspective, Brazilian scholars from the late nineteenth through the twentieth century focused on three broad factors in their studies of national development: Brazil's massive, largely unknown national territory; the country's relationship to the world economy; and the complex social structure of its multiracial population, particularly in the aftermath of abolition and the beginning of large-scale immigration from Europe, the Middle East, and Asia.

Gilberto Freyre (1900–87) was one of Brazil's foremost intellectuals whose work has been widely translated and admired worldwide. Freyre's complex and often disturbing ideas about the positive power of miscegenation promoted national pride among many Brazilians and were embraced by the Portuguese dictatorship to justify its continued colonial domination of Mozambique and Angola until the mid-1970s. Part of his appeal lay in the distinctions he drew between race relations in the United States and Brazil. Although raised in the city of Recife in the Northeast, he had been an undergraduate at Baylor University in Waco, Texas, beginning in 1917. He was a graduate student in Sociology at Columbia in the early 1920s and experienced firsthand the complexities of segregation in the United States, having studied in the deep South during Jim Crow and New York City during the Harlem Renaissance.

Freyre promoted the notion of "positive miscegenation." He believed that the combination of African, indigenous, and European peoples had created Brazilians who would genetically and socially embody all the best aspects of their various backgrounds. His benign descriptions of the ways this miscegenation happened ignored the power relations that allowed primarily Portuguese men to rape and control indigenous and Afro-Brazilian women. Freyre also embraced a type of eugenic thought that was increasingly popular in Latin America in the 1920s and 1930s. José Vasconcelos, the Mexican Minister of Education in the 1920s, argued that his nation benefited similarly through the presence of the so-called Cosmic Race made up of indigenous, African, European, and Asian people. Both Freyre and Vasconcelos were reacting against the elevation of European culture and whiteness that had been used to denigrate Latin Americans for so many years, but they did so by continuing to focus on the genetic backgrounds of their countries' populations rather than examining the actual structures and history that had shaped and continued to affect Brazil and Mexico.

A handful of Freyre's contemporaries examined Brazil's history, economy, and social structure, and focused their analyses on the nation's haphazard geographical and economic development. Rather than discussing racial and social traits, they identified Brazil's reliance on commodity exports and the resulting boom-and-bust economy as the root of many of the nation's ills. In 1936, Sérgio Buarque de Holanda published *Raízes do Brasil* (*Brazilian Roots*) and this was followed in 1942 by Caio Prado Júnior's *Formação do Brasil Contemporâneo* (*Formation of Contemporary Brazil*). These two scholars, in very different ways, focused on the legacy of Portuguese colonialism in the making of Brazil's unique geographical and economic development. Then, in 1958, Raimundo Faoro published *Os Donos de Poder* (*The Owners of Power*), which emphasized the continuity of authority, especially based in the planter class, from the colonial period through the twentieth century.

By the late 1950s and early 1960s, Brazilians began to question why theirs was not considered internationally one of the world's rising nations. There was a broad sense at home that the country was finally fulfilling its national motto of "Order and Progress." Everything from the opening of Brasília in 1960 to consecutive World Cup *futebol* victories in 1958 and 1962 brought great national pride and a sense that Brazil was on the cusp of greatness. But serious problems lay just beneath the surface. In 1964, the military overthrew the civilian government of João Goulart, and began a 21-year dictatorship. It was during this long period of authoritarianism that yet another generation of Brazilian intellectuals began to question the nature of their society. Emília Viotti da Costa (1928–2017) was a leading scholar of slavery who taught at the University of São Paulo before she was jailed for alleged subversion by the military government, and then physically removed from her post and forced into exile in the United States. Like Freyre before her, life at an American university – in her case, Yale – led da Costa to think comparatively about Brazil. She wrote a series of essays comparing land policies and economic and political liberalism in the United States and Brazil. Da Costa also directly challenged Freyre's benign sense of Brazil, unlike the United States, being a "racial democracy." These and other essays were eventually translated and published in English in 1985 as *The Brazilian Empire: Myths and Histories*.

Over the course of the long military dictatorship, Brazilian scholars, often writing in exile, analyzed their nation's past incomplete economic, social, and political development to try to break through many of the myths that da Costa and others identified. One scholar shifted the focus to the future by detailing the false promises of previous eras. Francisco Weffort (1937–2021), a São Paulo-based political scientist, wrote a brief treatise arguing that Brazil, even during long periods of civilian rule, had never been a democracy. *Por que Democracia?* (*Why Democracy?*) was published in 1984, just a year before the military left power. In the book, Weffort argues that for a system to be truly democratic, all the means and results of governance must be democratic. The book contained some of the central organizing ideals of the Workers' Party, which became a powerful force in Brazilian politics from the 1980s onward, producing two presidents (Luiz Inácio Lula da Silva, 2003–11 and 2023–, and Dilma Rousseff, 2011–16) along the way. Weffort's work not only influenced a political party on the rise, it also attempted to shunt aside the burdens of history by embracing democracy as a cure-all for the schisms in Brazilian society. Broad, participatory democracy, Weffort and many in the PT believed, was the key to making the nation whole.

From Capistrano de Abreu to Weffort, Brazilian intellectuals understood their nation as at best being in the process of making itself modern, and at worst woefully incomplete. The failure first of the Portuguese and then of successive Brazilian governments to control or even truly know the massive national territory was central to this failure. The ongoing legacy of racism, despite attempts by Freyre and his followers to write it away, further inhibited national development. And the long tradition of economic booms and busts tied to the production and export of commodities combined with these other factors to shape the country in ways that kept intellectuals, political leaders, businesspeople, and the military questioning how they could transform it into a modern coherent nation.

Brazil's Early Twenty-First Century of Euphoria and Despair

During the first decade of the twenty-first century, many Brazilians believed they had finally succeeded in creating the nation so many had imagined for so long. The first public expression of that belief came from abroad. In 2001, the investment bank Goldman Sachs published a widely disseminated and much-quoted report on the direction of the world economy in the new century, "Build Better Global Economic BRICS." It argued that the direction of the world economy in the future would be heavily influenced by and dependent upon the fortunes of the four BRIC countries, Brazil, Russia, India, and China. Although overly optimistic, the report resonated in Brazil, where the economy was growing and the political system seemed to be operating smoothly. Then the discovery of massive offshore oil deposits, hosting the FIFA World Cup in 2014 and then the 2016 Summer Olympics seemed to confirm Brazil's new-found status as a well-run country on the rise.

Development of the offshore oil and construction of facilities for the two mega-events ended up having the exact opposite impact on Brazil, however. Massive payoffs and other forms of corruption, along with a process of urban gentrification at the expense of poor and working-class Brazilians, revealed that the nation was not in the ideal position so many had imagined. Political chaos followed with the impeachment of one president, Dilma Rousseff, despite dubious charges against her, and the jailing of a former president, Luiz Inácio Lula da Silva, on even more questionable grounds. As Brazil headed toward the bicentennial of independence, its political system and economy were in disarray. Brazilians in many walks of life and from different political positions continue to vacillate between confidence in the future and frustration that their country cannot seem to fulfill its promise.

This book is a brief history of Brazil that focuses on the last two hundred years. History as a field often excels at nuance. Because this book is necessarily short, it often provides more context than nuance. That does not mean it is without an organizing thesis. The argument is that Brazil has struggled throughout its history to make itself into a nation state with a system of government that can peacefully reproduce itself and serve the broad interests of the population. It has been from its independence in 1822 to the present in a near constant state of trying to make itself into a coherent modern nation. There were ongoing attempts to embrace new export opportunities and to remake its population. There were certainly successes and failures, as there are in all nations. In Brazil, however, the frequent attempts to remake the nation took on a life of their own. And they were marked by a belief in the importance of both change and mobility. Despite, as noted above, its colonial history of having the bulk of its population "hug the coast like crabs," modern Brazil has been defined by movement and the belief that mobility would foster change and thus unify and make the nation modern.

The movement of people and goods, along with the opening of new areas to settlement and economic development, is part of the last two hundred years of Brazilian history. On both the national and state level, Brazilians have opened new capital cities since the late nineteenth century. There were solid political and economic reasons for building these, but they also represent the Brazilian tendency to look forward without much reference to the past. The national sense of hopefulness and belief in the idea that Brazil will be a leading nation in the near future is both empowering and problematic. On the positive side of the ledger, this set of beliefs has fostered bold and big ideas and projects from the creation of megadevelopment projects like the Itaipú Dam and Brasília itself to the radical restructuring of the energy sector with the creation of a nationwide ethanol program. The negative impact of such thinking has been a tendency to avoid confronting not only the past, but also present-day problems. That focus on the future left much undone in the making of the nation. This book explores that incomplete process from the arrival of the Portuguese court in 1808 through the bicentennial of independence in 2022 and the hotly contested national elections that followed.

1
Tropical Liberalism (1840–1930)

Brazilian independence came quickly and easily, especially when compared with most of the Americas. That smooth process served the immediate needs of Brazil's planter class, but postponed to some unknown future date many questions about state making, citizenship, and even the nature of what Brazil was to be as a nation. The two most important factors shaping 1822's independence from Portugal were the arrival of the royal court in 1808 and Brazil's near complete dependence on slavery as its dominant form of labor.

European geopolitics shaped the independence era throughout Latin America. In Brazil, they literally brought about its first iteration. Even before Napoleon Bonaparte invaded Spain in May 1808, Portugal's Braganza dynasty understood the threat the French Army posed to their reign. In November 1807, they arranged to move most of the royal court to Brazil. Under the protection of the British Navy, the Portuguese monarchs and many of their advisors and hangers-on arrived in South America on January 22, 1808, instantly transforming Brazil from colony to metropole. Dom João VI ruled the Portuguese Empire from Rio de Janeiro from 1808 (although he only formally became king in 1816) until his return to

Portugal in 1821 to take control of the volatile political situation there. The Portuguese monarch left his son, Dom Pedro I, in charge of Brazil. Planters sought to push this arrangement even further, and encouraged Pedro to sever ties with Lisbon and make Brazil independent. On January 9, 1822, Pedro complied and declared, "As it is for the good of all and the general happiness of the Nation, I am ready. Tell the People that I will stay. I stay!" After receiving news from Portugal rejecting this move in September 1822, Pedro, while in Ipiranga, São Paulo, declared, "For my blood, my honor, my God, I swear to give Brazil freedom. . . . Brazilians, Independence or Death!" This declaration of independence is known as the Cry of Ipiringa (*Grito de Inpiranga*), and September 7 has since been celebrated as Brazilian independence day.

This transition guaranteed the political stability that allowed for ongoing economic growth. And by keeping the monarchy in place and firmly established in Brazil itself, there was little to no chance of a political revolution or other challenge to the status quo. Given that, slavery would remain the dominant form of labor for the foreseeable future. Beyond the maintenance of slavery and support for commodity production and export, Brazilian independence included no clearly articulated program for national development. Planters remained the most powerful actors in Brazil. Even though they had pushed Pedro to declare independence, many of them did not trust the Brazilian emperor, who maintained close ties to his father back in Portugal. The planters' power and the absence of any sort of national political project combined to deepen the regionalism that had defined much of the colonial era.

Creating a Brazilian Empire

Pedro I was the ideal figure to lead Brazilian independence, but he was hardly equipped to craft the new nation's politics. He eventually acquiesced to the idea of governing with a constitution in place, and so an elected assembly began to work on that document starting in May 1823. Assembly members wanted to codify a system of complete free trade, but Pedro continued to have an affinity for Portugal. The monarch was so put off by this and other disagreements that he dissolved the assembly and exiled its leaders in November 1823. He then wrote the constitution himself. Not surprisingly, it concentrated power in his hands despite formally having three separate branches of government. Pedro also appointed the states' governors (known then as "provincial presidents"), further centralizing power in his hands in Rio. All of these moves alienated the powerful planter class.

Brazil was weak economically at this time, and totally dependent on trade with Great Britain and Portugal. Pedro was not unaware of the growing discontent among planters, so in 1831 he appointed a new cabinet that was completely made up of Brazilian-born men. He did so to mollify the planters he had been alienating for nine years, but the new cabinet only highlighted the distant and personalistic nature of Pedro's nine years as emperor. With no improvement in sight, he abdicated and returned to Portugal soon after the new cabinet was seated. He left behind his five-year-old son, Pedro II, who would become Brazil's emperor when he reached the age of majority on his eighteenth birthday. Until Pedro II could rule, Brazil operated under a system known as the Regency. A three-man panel governed the country in the young monarch's name. They were also responsible for training Pedro II to become the nation's leader. Unlike his father, who had been born and initially educated in Portugal, the younger Pedro would be a completely Brazilian leader by the time his eighteenth birthday arrived.

During the Regency (1831–40), Brazilian planters finally had direct control of the national government. And although the Regency was the national government, the planters who ran it were primarily interested in maintaining their power, which meant local control at Rio's expense. They also had little interest in altering the nation's reliance on slavery. Politically, they embraced a regionalism that privileged planters throughout the nation over the central state in Rio. That diffusion of power undermined any sense of Brazil as a coherent nation, and bred broad discontent with the status quo, especially in regions far from the capital. Between 1832 and 1838, there were five major rebellions in these areas. They were often made up of multiracial coalitions of people who rejected the established order, and wanted to be even more independent from Rio. Some rebellions sought relief from the power of the local planters, while others pushed to separate completely from Brazil. Although none succeeded, collectively they created a crisis for the men running Regency, who reacted with a bold and in some ways absurd move: they declared that the 14-year-old Pedro II was, for the purposes of governing Brazil, legally 18.

On July 23, 1840, Brazil's political leaders declared that Pedro II had reached the age of majority four years early. His ascendance calmed the political situation, finally completed the process of making the government fully Brazilian, and began a truly national period of governance that would challenge, to some degree, the Regency's extreme federalism. Pedro II ruled using the 1824 constitution, and took on the role as the moderating power between rival Liberal and Conservative political factions. Once again, Brazil experienced a major political transformation peacefully and without popular mobilization behind an agenda for the political and/or economic development of the nation. This precluded the creation of a political system capable of responding to the needs and aspirations of the majority of the nation's people. But even at only 14 years of age, Pedro II was much more prepared than his father or the leaders of the Regency to rule Brazil. And although he had no discernible program, he would prove to be the ideal leader for Brazil as its economy began to flourish when it became the world's greatest producer and exporter of coffee.

From the time Pedro II became emperor until the advent of the Great Depression in 1930, the Brazilian economy grew steadily through the export of coffee, rubber, and other commodities. The macro-level political peace during Pedro II's reign (1840–89) and the Old Republic (1889–1930) that followed it greatly facilitated the ongoing growth of the export economy. That stability began at the top. Pedro's biographers often described him as "calm," "deliberate," and "serious." He projected that personality in portraits and official photographs by appearing in austere-looking black suits. In an era before mass communications, Pedro set out to be a calming and dominant symbol of the Brazilian nation. As a ruler, he was strict, but not an absolutist, because he had been taught by his tutors during the Regency the importance of balancing the nation's various regional interests. When he assumed the throne as a 14 year old, he relied heavily on advisors, but his education and training prepared him so well that he took charge by the time he was in his early twenties.

The plantation remained the primary organizing unit for both the economy and the political system. Formal politics operated with Pedro as the ultimate moderating authority over the elected National Assembly, which was made up of wealthy adult males primarily tied to the agricultural economy. Pedro also worked with an appointed cabinet known as the

Council of State, which had no formal power, but that allowed the monarch to balance regional and other interests. As in most Latin American nations in the nineteenth century, Brazilian politics were dominated by members of the Liberal and Conservative parties. Unlike in Mexico, where that division eventually led to a civil war and French occupation, Brazilian Liberals and Conservatives were not far apart politically. The parties were defined more by their geographical bases. Landowners from areas in decline, such as Bahia in the Northeast, tended to be Conservatives, while those from more economically dynamic areas (São Paulo, Minas Gerais, Rio Grande do Sul) were Liberals. Many bureaucrats in Rio were members of the Conservative party, while other urban professionals tended to be Liberals.

Liberals often sought to diffuse power back to the provinces, while Conservatives usually opposed that. Pedro balanced these interests by moving back and forth between Liberal and Conservative cabinets. During the 49 years of his reign, he had 36 different cabinets. The longest lasting was in place from early 1871 to mid-1875. The shortest lasted only six days in 1862. In all, Liberals held the cabinet for 17 years, three months, and 28 days; Conservatives for 20 years, eight months, and 19 days. The remaining were mixed cabinets. This balance seems to validate the Visconde de Albuqurque's comment that "there was nothing so like a Conservative as a Liberal in power." That was because both parties' leaders, no matter what their differences on individual policies, promoted the interests of large landowners and the maintenance of slavery.

This political structure reflected the nation's long history of export booms and busts. As mentioned in the introduction, the nation got its name from the first commodity it exported to Europe, brazilwood. Sugar (in the Northeast) quickly fueled the export economy as Brazil grew as a colony. Sugar was followed by gold and diamond exports from the Center-South province of Minas Gerais during the colonial era. There was a short-lived cotton boom centered in the Northeast while US cotton production plummeted during the American Civil War, and a longer Amazonian rubber boom from the 1850s until the British successfully harvested plantation-grown rubber in Malaysia in the early 1900s.

During the first few decades after independence, sugar continued to be Brazil's most valuable commodity, accounting for about a third of total exports. Sugar prices began to decline, however, as Caribbean producers, along with the European and later US-based sugar beet industry, glutted the market. Even with a steadily increasing world demand for sugar, Brazilian producers' fortunes were in decline by mid-century as they could not compete on price. Declining sugar prices affected Brazil's Northeast more than any other region, and ultimately helped the coffee economy in the nation's Center-South take off, beginning in the 1830s, as Northeastern planters sold their slaves to their counterparts in Rio de Janeiro and São Paulo. Coffee came to dominate the economy and within a decade Brazil was the world's leading producer. Indeed, it has remained a mainstay of the nation's agriculture exports into the twenty-first century.

Coffee, Slavery, and Nation Building

Brazil's coffee economy has undergone several phases. The first coffee boom began in the 1830s in the Paraíba Valley in the state of Rio de Janeiro. European and American demand for coffee grew exponentially at this time, and Brazil's planters used every bit of available land, including hillsides, to cultivate the crop. They brought in as many African slaves as possible to work their coffee plantations. While some slaves continued to be forcibly taken from the homeland in Africa and shipped to the Americas, the slave trade was increasingly limited by the British Navy, which sought to enforce a ban, beginning in 1807. Although Brazil formally removed itself from the Atlantic slave trade in 1831, illegal shipments of human beings from Africa continued until the British Navy moved to end all such activity by 1850, when the slave trade was near its peak for Brazil. These limits forced coffee planters to purchase slaves from the declining sugar plantations in the Northeast.

Coffee production drove a dramatic increase in overall exports. From 1833 to the end of the Empire in 1889, the value of all Brazilian exports grew sevenfold.

Although the rubber boom took place during these years, the dramatic growth in exports was driven by coffee. It had accounted for less than 20% of a much smaller total in 1822, and was responsible for almost 70% of a much bigger total of exports in 1889. Coffee was so valuable to Brazil that the nation ran a trade surplus beginning in 1860. Its impact on the country was broad. Coffee production led to the introduction of the nation's first railroads and brought great wealth to the nation's Center-South region. Coffee would even play a role in Brazil's early industrialization. By the late nineteenth century, the country was responsible for between 80 and 90% of the world's coffee exports and so it used the vast majority of the world's cotton jute coffee sacks. Cotton producers from the Northeast and entrepreneurs in São Paulo and Rio de Janeiro moved – with the help of tariffs on imported cotton textiles and government support for the importation of spinning and weaving equipment – to establish a national textile industry that would help fuel the creation of the country's industrial sector.

In many ways, coffee laid the foundation for the rise of Brazil's modern economy, despite its continued reliance on slave labor. At the most basic level, it created a great deal of wealth that remained in the country. The British dominated the coffee trade at first, but Brazil's two largest markets were the world's two biggest coffee consumers, the United States and Germany. Wealthy Brazilians, controlling the land and production, were able to profit directly from these coffee exports. Often, other Latin American countries' export sectors, where mines and plantations were foreign-owned, did not produce as much wealth for their local economies.

The steady growth in export revenue led Brazilian authorities to write laws and create institutions to facilitate trade, regularize the currency and foreign exchange, and promote broad economic growth. They wrote a series of commercial codes in the 1840s and founded a central bank, the Bank of Brazil, in 1851. At the same time, local political and business leaders opened a series of regional banks. Pedro's government next began to create political and cultural institutions to promote a Brazilian identity. The 1874 opening of the National Library (Biblioteca Nacional) was the most obvious example of this new focus. These developments, along with the expansion of telegraph lines and railroads, and the establishment of steamship travel up the Amazon River, were important, concrete examples of the few attempts at nation building since Pedro I's 1822 declaration of independence.

Planters in the Paraíba Valley were so eager to profit from expanding world demand for coffee that they planted the crop everywhere, without regard to the environmental impact of such practices. Their irresponsible land use affected productivity, and led future planters to move to the much more fecund lands in the state of São Paulo. Although slavery remained the dominant labor system when coffee moved into São Paulo, the high profits it generated, along with the expense of relying on slave labor after the international slave trade had ended, began the slow process of moving toward free wage labor in Brazil. Brazilian planters had long relied on the ongoing importation of new slaves because the extraordinarily harsh ways they treated their slaves resulted in high mortality rates.

Brazil's size and economic diversity, even in the nineteenth century, led to differing conditions for slaves in different settings. Some slaves who had skills that were highly valued throughout society, such as carpentry, sewing, and so forth, were hired out by their masters. These urban slaves were sometimes able to create for themselves separate spaces, and so could live some aspects of their lives outside the master–slave relationship by working for wages not collected by their masters. These men and women even formed their own associations that provided a decent burial and, in some cases, could provide assistance for slaves to buy their own freedom. These urban folk were a small portion of the total slave population, however. The vast majority of slaves worked in agriculture, and had extraordinarily harsh and brief lives. During much of the nineteenth century, the average life expectancy for an African brought against their will to Brazil was only seven years after arrival. The horrible conditions created by the planters themselves meant that the end of the international slave trade profoundly affected those Brazilian planters' labor supply and ability to produce and export commodities.

The shift in coffee production to São Paulo beginning in the 1870s stirred the beginnings of abolitionist thought in Brazil. Some slavery opponents did so for moral reasons, but a steadily increasing number of forward-looking Brazilian businessmen began to question the economic efficacy of maintaining slavery. There were also deeply racist reasons for some abolitionist politics. Brazilian intellectuals increasingly embraced eugenic thought, and began to argue that the country's massive population of people of color would retard national progress. These political leaders, businessmen, and intellectuals sought to literally whiten the population through European immigration. But they knew that white immigrants were loath to come to Brazil to work alongside slaves. To spur European immigration, these leaders sought to end slavery.

All of these developments helped to create a distinct sense of Brazilian nationalism under Pedro II. Related to that was the idea that Brazil needed to finally address questions about what exactly constituted the nation. Debates about slavery and European immigration shaped the social component of those issues, but questions about where exactly Brazil's national territory ended in the North and the West were also increasingly being asked. At the same time, many Brazilian elites began to feel a sense of economic and political competition with Argentina. Indeed, there had been ongoing conflicts since the colonial era about control of the Rio de la Plata. The river's headwaters were firmly in Brazilian territory, but Uruguay and Argentina controlled access to the sea. The growing Argentine–Brazilian competition increasingly revolved around control of the river.

Landlocked Paraguay was literally and figuratively in the middle of all of this. Fearing for its national survival, Paraguay built the largest and best-equipped military in South America. To attempt to gain control over the river that was so important for Paraguay's internal and foreign trade, it invaded the Brazilian state of Mato Grosso in 1865, after having ended Brazil's access to the river in November 1864. Pedro and his military advisors decided to put aside their fears of an increasingly dominant Argentina and formed an alliance with Argentina and Uruguay to fight the powerful Paraguay river-based Navy and its assertive Army. The so-called War of the Triple Alliance or Paraguayan War began on May 1, 1865, and lasted until March 1870.

The war ravaged Paraguay, which had been a successful, mixed-race society that despite its small size had fought off the combined forces of the Argentine, Brazilian, and Uruguayan militaries for five years. Even though it was victorious, however, Brazil was also profoundly impacted by the war, losing between 33,000 and 50,000 men in battle. The wide range in the estimate is yet another reminder of the weak national government at this time, which had a far from complete understanding of what exactly was transpiring in the conflict. But the war itself began the process of changing that. The Brazilian military started the process of becoming a key national institution during the conflict. Before 1865, Pedro had relied on mercenaries to put down regional rebellions. The war also jolted some Brazilian leaders, including the emperor, out of their complacency about the nation's weak national development. Brazil's military leadership understood how Paraguay's powerful domestic industry, which had largely been developed by shunning the world trading system that shaped the Brazilian political economy, propped up its war effort. Paraguay could fight a protracted conflict against three other nations because it could produce many of its own weapons and ships. Seeing that firsthand, Brazilian military and political leaders began to raise the issue of the nation's development. They questioned their ongoing reliance on foreign economic interests and the maintenance of a weak central state. Pedro himself reflected on this in letters he wrote home from his tour of the United States during its centennial celebration in 1876. After reviewing the impressive displays of American-made machines exhibited in Philadelphia's Fairmont Park, he could not help but remark that the United States was barely a decade past the abolition of slavery and yet was already a major industrial power.

Pedro failed to understand the nuances of North American economic development and the fact that industry was flourishing in areas that had long ago abolished slavery, but he did inadvertently touch upon questions of slavery and national economic development in Brazil. He did this just after the Paraguayan war had directly affected the ongoing viability of slavery. Any enslaved Brazilian who fought in the war was granted their freedom. While only 6,000 men gained their freedom this way, the fact that these veterans became free Brazilian citizens in exchange for serving the nation altered, at least a little at first, the ways race and nation were connected. Moreover, after the war, some Brazilian military leaders bristled at the suggestion that their troops should be involved in chasing and capturing runaway slaves.

It was in this political atmosphere in 1870 that intellectuals, politicians, and businessmen founded a series of state-based Republican parties, which would eventually take over politics after the 1889 fall of the Empire. Abolitionists were also increasingly assertive at this time and many among the rising officer corps embraced Positivism (a belief that a society needed to be well ordered to achieve progress) as a guiding philosophy, and in some cases a religion. Republicanism, abolitionism, and Positivism intersected in some ways, but what truly tied them together was how new and separate they were from the ideas espoused by Brazil's old landholding elites. These newer ideas helped to define the rising agricultural and business interests in the period after the Paraguayan War, particularly among the elites of São Paulo, the Paulistas.

Political pressure grew to end slavery as a growing number of Paulista planters, military men, and urban intellectuals looked to the eventual establishment of free wage labor and the beginnings of mass European immigration. Many enslaved Brazilians hastened that process by escaping into the interior to join runaway slave communities known as *quilombos*. Other people used the complexity of slave codes to gain their freedom or try to ameliorate the harsh conditions of their lives. They largely succeeded in making the maintenance of slavery more costly and complex. Pedro's government began to enact laws that signaled slavery's end. As early as 1850, the Queiróz Law had outlawed Brazil's participation in the African slave trade, thus recognizing that slavery would eventually disappear. The 1871 Free Womb Law or Rio Branco Law laid the legal framework for slavery's slow demise. Children born to slaves were technically free, and could be completely free at age eight if an indemnity were paid. If not, they became free of any obligations at age 21. In 1885, the Saraiva–Cotegipe Law granted freedom to all people over the age of 60. Of course, given the brutality of Brazilian slavery, only a small number lived long enough for this law to affect them.

These laws were political expressions of the work of slaves, abolitionists, and others to end the institution. Princess Isabel, Pedro's daughter, announced the Golden Law ending slavery on May 13, 1888. As momentous as this was, abolition was more a reflection of reality than a major change in society. At independence in 1822, about half of Brazil's four million people were slaves. In 1888, with a population of 14 million, there were less than three-quarters of a million slaves, or just 5% of Brazilians. While the nation's elites had depended on slavery for most of the nineteenth century, many of them now blamed it for Brazil's lack of progress compared to the United States and many European nations. Abolition did nothing to erase the deep racism upon which slavery rested. Miscegenation was widely embraced as a way to transform the population and make it whiter. Even as intellectuals and politicians dreamed of creating a whiter populace, they did not give much thought to the question of what made someone Brazilian.

The "Fall" of the Monarchy and the Creation of a Republic

Up until 1889, most people in Brazil were simply considered subjects of the Portuguese and then Brazilian monarchy. The state-based Republican parties focused more on moving away from monarchy than on the creation of citizenship rights for the majority of the nation's people. In fact, the Army spearheaded the push to bring down the monarchy. These leaders had formed the Clube Militar in 1886, and it increasingly advocated for political change to aid national development along Positivist and Republican lines. And so it was not a complete surprise when, on November 15, 1889, Marshal Deodoro da Fonseca (the head of the Armed Forces) informed Pedro II that the Empire was at an end. The Army had surrounded the Palace and declared

Brazil to be a republic. As had been the case with independence from Portugal in 1822, there was no broad mobilization or popular calls for a particular form of government. For the majority of Brazilians, little changed after the Empire fell.

Historians have long used the passive voice to describe the regime as "falling" to emphasize the absence of popular mobilization or the push for a new governmental program. With the end of slavery, there did not seem to be any reason to remain a monarchy, and so institutions such as the military, Church, and planter class simply withdrew their support for Pedro's rule. That simple explanation, while correct, obscures the complicated nexus between abolitionism and republicanism in late nineteenth-century Brazil. The abolition movement helped foster the development of republicanism. At first, that connection was a positive one as the two movements complemented each other. The timing and interconnected nature of these two reveal the ways citizenship rights were shaped by race. After the fall of the Empire, political leaders did not attempt to grant full citizenship rights to ex-slaves. Instead, as noted in the introduction, they attempted to erase slavery from the nation's past by burning records related to it and calling for increases in European immigration. Abolitionism and republicanism were seen as two separate but related ideas. One would end slavery and the other would create a republic, but really primarily for white people. The failure to connect the two meant that in many ways the end of slavery ended up deepening many of the most racist aspects of Brazilian society.

The Republic began with military rule. Deodoro da Fonseca took control of the government, and military men ran 10 of the nation's 20 states. Although civilians manned the cabinet, the military's leadership and many in Rio saw it as the only truly national institution capable of governing Brazil. The Catholic Church, a transnational institution with roots in a line of authority tied to Europe, could not fill the vacuum left by the end of the monarchy despite having a national presence. The Army was really the most national institution in Brazil, but it was barely present in most of the country. Its coming to power ultimately destabilized politics and led to a period of chaotic federalism that initially undermined the early Republic.

The balance of power between the national government in Rio de Janeiro and the states had plagued Brazil since independence. The need to centralize authority in the national capital was a key driver in the decision to make Pedro II a legal adult as a 14 year old. As the emperor, Pedro served as a moderating force among planters from different regions. The Republic attempted to replicate that arrangement, but with the military hierarchy in charge. Centralized command and control, which is fundamental to military discipline and operations, was completely antithetical to the interests of Brazil's far-flung and varied members of the planter class. A series of regional uprisings and even divisions within the military made that apparent to all. Deodoro at first reacted to this instability by closing the legislature (the National Assembly) and then working to quell a schism with the Navy. He finally simply resigned in 1891, two years after assuming power. Floriano Peixoto, the vice president and another military man, assumed the presidency, but without a well-defined mandate.

Peixoto served for three years, until November 1894. Given the chaotic state of affairs during his reign, he ceded power to a representative of Brazil's most powerful planters. Prudente José de Morais e Barros, a lawyer from the interior of São Paulo, won Brazil's first presidential election as a representative of the Paulista Republican Party. His ascension to power marked the beginning of a long period of macro-level political peace dominated by the Republican parties of Brazil's two richest and most productive states, São Paulo and Minas Gerais. The former was the nation's leading coffee producer and the latter a major dairy state. Their dominance from 1894 to 1930 came to be known as the era of "*a política de café com leite*," or "the politics of coffee with milk." Indeed, a conflict between the two over presidential succession led to fall of the Republic in 1930.

Tensions between local and national interests festered under the military and civilian governments of the Republic. During Floriano Peixoto's brief tenure, the national government had to contend with a military uprising in Brazil's southernmost state, Rio

Grande do Sul, and another regional rebellion in the southern state of Santa Catarina. After Prudente de Morais took office, a millenarian rebellion in the interior of the Northeast state of Bahia rocked the nation. The Canudos Rebellion involved tens of thousands of poor people who had migrated to the interior of Bahia in the face of an ongoing drought. They built a new religious community that rejected both the Republic and Brazil's Catholic hierarchy. The state's planters feared that such a massive migration would make agricultural labor scarce. That and the ways the people in Canudos rejected both state and federal authority led Bahia's leaders to send the state militia to destroy the community. After the locals soundly defeated the state forces, the federal government sent an ever-escalating series of Army contingents to subdue the revolt. Although the government in Rio eventually beat the rebels and destroyed Canudos, the entire episode revealed the central state's and military's weaknesses. It also made obvious to people throughout the nation that elites in Rio and other cities lived in completely different worlds than most rural Brazilians.

Another millenarian uprising, this time in the southern states of Santa Catarina and Paraná between 1912 and 1916, demonstrated yet again the social, economic, and political differences between urban and rural Brazilians. During the Contestado Rebellion, federal troops again were sent long distances through rough terrain to subdue an uprising of peasants.

This time, the latter's opposition to the Republic and the intrusion of outsiders building a railroad led to an outright war with the national government. The soldiers were not only foreign to the peasants, even landowners who supported the Army's intervention did not feel at home with the outsiders. Several landowners admitted that they had never before seen the national flag or heard the national anthem when the assembled troops played it on a gramophone.

Brazil's massive size and underdeveloped infrastructure figured prominently in the rise and eventual destruction of both the Canudos and Contestado uprisings. Military leaders noted that the absence of physical, economic, and social connections between the nation's coastal cities and its interior had not only helped to foster these rebellions, they made it incredibly difficult for the Army to respond to them. A great deal of early developmentalist thought among military men began in this period. Those officers not only criticized the ways Brazil's export economy had focused infrastructure in those areas that produced coffee, sugar, and other commodities, they also began to discuss how they felt Brazil's population should be remade in order for the nation to become truly modern. Those same military men would begin to play a significant role in national politics when they began to articulate a new vision of a more unified Brazil.

Their critique of national development – that so much of it was simply in response to commodity production and export – was not far off the mark. The city of São Paulo had been a backwater from the colonial period through the late nineteenth century. It grew dramatically as coffee flourished in the state's interior, but São Paulo's eventual industrial development was an exception to the pattern of Brazilian urban growth. Brazil's late nineteenth-century rubber boom revealed how this process worked in the nation's far north. Rubber was collected by tappers (*seringueiros*), who tended to work alone. Middlemen moved the rubber from the far-flung tappers to the Amazonian cities of Manaus and Belém. The latter sits at the Atlantic mouth of the Amazon River, the former at the intersection of the Solimões and Rio Negro rivers.

International demand for rubber in the mid-nineteenth century and the advent of steamship travel on the Amazon in 1852 began the transformation of both cities. Before steam-based travel, the 900-mile voyage from Belém on the Atlantic to Manaus in the interior took two months for a sailing vessel, but only one month for the return trip with the current's help. Steamships made it up the river in only nine days, with the return trip taking only four. By 1855, there was a regular service between Belém and Manaus, and that dramatically accelerated rubber exports and urban development. In 1840, Brazil exported 388 tons of rubber. One decade later, the number rose to 1,467 tons, and by 1860 it reached 2,700 tons. The region's overall population grew accordingly, with Manaus and Belém expanding dramatically. In 1875, it had roughly 40,000 residents, with this number growing to around 100,000 in 1900. Manaus also became the first Brazilian city with a comprehensive electric lighting system. It had a modern waterworks and extensive garbage collection. The Manaus Opera House stands to this day as the city's most obvious symbol of late nineteenth-century affluence and, in some important ways, waste.

Urbanization, Immigration, and New Political Challenges

The export economy also drove the creation of a new state capital in Minas Gerais in Brazil's Center-South. Belo Horizonte opened in 1897 as a planned city that the state's elites hoped would unify their disparate agricultural interests so their state could better compete with São Paulo's planters. Belo helped the state's coffee planters, dairy interests, and mining concerns coordinate public policy and spending to promote internal development and expand exports. The new state capital foreshadowed what would become a Brazilian tradition of attempting to alter national development in the interior with urban development. Henry Ford famously tried in the 1930s and early 1940s to create rubber plantations for tire manufacture for his automobile company. While both Fordlândia and the much larger Belterra were failures, they did transform parts of the Amazonian state of Pará. At about the same time, political leaders in the interior state of Goiás founded a new planned capital city, Goiâna, in 1933.

Although most pronounced in the nation's interior, Brazil's cities were not immune from the widening social, economic, and political divides in society. Those divisions burst into the national consciousness in Rio de Janeiro in 1904 when many poor and working-class Cariocas (residents of the city) rose up and rioted against plans to forcibly vaccinate them against yellow fever. For four days, people destroyed trolleys, street lamps, and other symbols of Rio's modernity. While millenarian uprisings far from the major cities on the coast worried elites, they could be dismissed as the irrational actions of people who had not had much contact with what they saw as Brazilian civilization. These urban riots highlighted the stark divisions even within Brazil's most modern and outward-looking city.

The success of Brazil's agricultural economy led to the growth of many of its cities. Just as rubber exports had funded urban development in Manaus and Belém, Rio de Janeiro flourished along with the expanding national economy. Mineiros (residents of Monas Gerais) had celebrated the strength of their economy by opening Belo Horizonte as their new state capital in 1897. But no Brazilian city prospered and expanded during the first decades of the twentieth century as much as São Paulo. And that growth was driven by Brazil's expanding coffee economy, which was increasingly centered in São Paulo.

Paulista planters had the advantage of being the second group of Brazilian coffee producers. The first coffee boom, as we saw above, was centered in the Paraíba Valley in the state of Rio de Janeiro. European and North American demand for coffee brought environmental degradation and a shift in slave ownership from the Northeast to the Center-South. Coffee in the state of Rio de Janeiro was incredibly profitable, but the planters, rush to increase production hit several considerable bottlenecks. Relying on slave labor was costly in a number of interconnected ways. With the international slave trade outlawed, Rio's planters had to import slaves from other Brazilian regions at considerable cost. Moreover, slaves were not passive sources of docile labor. They were captive and brutalized, but they could also resist aspects of their harsh conditions through subtle forms of sabotage and slowdowns in the fields. Enslaved Brazilians also increasingly used the court system when they could to mitigate the worst of their conditions. A not insignificant number of people also fled when they could to runaway slave communities in Brazil's interior. These informal towns became key sites of exchange among interior folk (including many indigenous Brazilians) and runaway slaves, and also played a role in fostering trade between the interior and the coast.

Coffee bushes can take a decade from the time they are planted to when they produce berries that can be harvested. Given the experience of planters in the Paraíba Valley, Paulistas were much more careful with their land management, and even created state-sponsored extension services to promote the agricultural sector. Also, given their investment in coffee came as slavery was increasingly being challenged by Brazilian abolitionists and the slaves themselves, Paulista planters tried to move on to free wage labor for coffee cultivation. That impulse, along with the increasing embrace of eugenic theories about the supposed superiority of white Europeans over people from the rest of the world, pushed Paulista elites to embrace immigration as a source of labor for the agricultural sector. European immigrants in the mid- to late nineteenth century had a number of destinations in the Western Hemisphere without slavery, making Brazil an unattractive destination.

Slave resistance, abolitionist politics, modernizing Paulista planters, and the Brazilian military's increasing distaste for the institution led to the eventual end of slavery. As was noted above, Princess Isabel, Dom Pedro II's daughter, announced the so-called Golden Law ending slavery in Brazil on May 13, 1888. This opened the door for Paulista planters to initiate a large-scale immigration program. From 1908 through 1936, 1,221,282 immigrants entered Brazil through the Paulista port of Santos. Italian, Portuguese, Spanish, and other families came to São Paulo to work in the coffee sector as so-called *colonos*. They were given a house and coffee trees to cultivate. They were also permitted to grow additional crops that they could sell themselves. Coffee *colonos* became a de facto agricultural middle class in Brazil, and they played a significant role in São Paulo's economic growth. The state also brought in 176,775 Japanese immigrants during these years to grow vegetables, raise chickens, and do other agricultural labor to help feed the growing cities. These dual immigration programs shared a number of characteristics, such as their focus on agriculture and their reliance on bringing immigrant families intact to Brazil. They were also planned, implemented, and financed by the state of São Paulo without the participation of the federal government in Rio.

São Paulo's immigration policies highlighted a central feature of the highly federated nature of Brazilian politics during the Old Republic: the states were the primary actors in most policies, and there were significant differences in the finances and capacity of the various states. São Paulo was, by far, the richest in Brazil, and its policies reflected that. Another clear example of Paulista policy was the 1906–14 Coffee Valorization program, which boosted prices in the face of modest international demand. The state's planters petitioned the national government in Rio for support, but were turned down. The state then sought out international financing for a program that bought and destroyed excess coffee stocks, even using some of the beans as fuel for locomotives. Paulista planters used the power of state spending to prop up the agricultural sector, but they did so on their own given the limited nature and perspective of the national government.

On the surface, the politics and economics of the Old Republic functioned well. There were localized rebellions and strikes, but there seemed to be macro-level political peace. Steady economic growth, based primarily on commodity exports, undergirded that political tranquility. Events in the late 1910s and early 1920s challenged that façade of political peace, however. A series of general strikes, first in São Paulo in 1917 and then in Rio in 1919, brought disorder to Brazil's two largest and most economically dynamic cities. While the participants in millenarian uprisings could be dismissed as "backward" rural folk, the striking workers were often either European immigrants or their children who worked in industries that elites considered advanced and a key to Brazil becoming a modern nation. Those widespread industrial strikes were in some ways a precursor to a broader rejection of the status quo by segments of the middle class and elite who were not directly connected to the export of agricultural commodities.

The two Tenente Rebellions by young army officers in Rio and São Paulo in 1922 and 1924, along with the avant-garde Week of Modern Art in 1922, signaled that significant segments of politically active Brazilians increasingly questioned and even rejected the liberal economic order. These critiques of the establishment specifically called out the nation's failure to function as something more than a loose collection of states and regions that had their own separate relationships to their export markets. Although their protests were public and well known, they had little impact on politics throughout the 1920s. The booming world economy, particularly in the primary markets for Brazilian coffee and other commodities in North America and Western Europe, helped maintain the status quo. Change would only come through a traditional political crisis of clashing regional interests around the standing of various state governors in the 1930 presidential election.

Throughout most of the Old Republic, the political leaders from Brazil's two most powerful states, São Paulo and Minas Gerais, alternated as the nation's president, although others did serve when this arrangement broke down. Paulista Washington Luís (1926–30) broke this tradition and attempted to deny the Mineiro governor the opportunity to lead Brazil by supporting his protégé from São Paulo, Júlio Prestes, in the 1930 election. This move brought an immediate backlash from most of the governors of the other states, who ended up backing governor Getúlio Vargas, a Gaúcho (someone from Brazil's southern-most state, Rio Grande do Sul), for president. Although the vote total was closer than usual, Prestes won the 1930 presidential election. The old ways of the politics of the governors at first seemed secure. It turned out that they were not. The developing economic depression, along with years of ferment among younger military men and intellectuals, provided the basis for what would become the Revolution of 1930, which would represent the first sustained challenge to the liberal economic order, as well as the first serious attempt to knit together Brazil's disparate regions and states into a coherent nation.

2
The Failed March to Modernity (1930–1964)

Until the late 1929 Wall Street crash, the 1920s were a deceptively calm decade in Brazil. Commodity prices remained strong, with coffee and sugar reaching new highs in 1927, and the ongoing trading of the presidency between the governors of São Paulo and Minas Gerais continued. On the surface, the liberal economic order and patriarchal political system continued to promote macro-level economic growth. So it is ironic that a squabble between the political leaders of those two states over who would become Brazil's next president in 1930 led to the dismantling of the entire political system, and the first real challenge to the liberal economic order. The Revolution of 1930, as it became known, was the beginning of Brazil's attempts to create a modern, socially and geographically integrated, and economically diversified nation. From 1930 to 1964, through dictatorship and democracy, a new group of Brazilian leaders used the central state to foster industrialization, attempt to gain control over the vast national territory, and try to incorporate the majority of the population into the political system.

When President Washington Luís (1926–30) pushed to have his political protégé from São Paulo,

Júlio Prestes, named the candidate of the dominant Republican Party, the governors of several states, included Minas Gerais, objected and made Getúlio Vargas, the governor of Brazil's southern-most state, Rio Grande do Sul, the leader of an opposition state. While Vargas lost the election, a series of political machinations led him to spearhead a rebellion of military men and politicians throughout the nation. The quick capitulation by Washington Luís made the Revolution of 1930 a largely bloodless coup. The movement had no real program beyond preventing the Paulistas from retaining control of the presidency. It would be up to Vargas and his supporters to determine how Brazil would face the challenges brought on by the Great Depression.

The onset of the Depression quickly affected all of Latin America. Dramatic drops in commodity prices brought on challenges from the political right and left throughout the region. Vargas was unique in this context because he came to power without a clear agenda. Over the course of the 1930s and 1940s, he ruled as a provisional president, a fascist-style dictator, and a proto-populist. After being removed by the military in 1945, he returned to the political scene as a senator, and then he won the 1950 presidential election. One factor unifies all the different Vargas types of rule over these years: he was Brazil's first modern leader, and he ushered in a long experiment with modernity that sought to transform the nation from a simple commodity producer to a more geographically and socially unified and economically diverse nation.

Centralizing Power in Rio de Janeiro

Upon taking office in late 1930, Vargas set about to strengthen Rio's hand in national politics. He quickly created new institutions and moved to write a constitution that would embody this new orientation. It was a modernist document. The 1934 Constitution included women's suffrage and a mandated minimum wage, although both of these would not be in effect for most of Vargas's initial period of rule. His first big institutional move was to create the Ministry of Labor, Industry, and Commerce in 1931 to promote national economic development. Popularly known simply as the Ministry of Labor, this new governmental body did in fact seek to take over the nation's fledgling unions and completely regulate industrial relations, but it also attempted to promote industry and trade. It had as its over-arching goal the creation of a new assertive role for the federal government in Rio over the economic affairs of the nation.

This new Ministry of Labor faced its first test in 1931 when workers in a number of factories in São Paulo, Brazil's industrial hub, struck for higher wages. Vargas had replaced a number of state governors with former *tenentes* – the young military officers who had gone into revolt in 1922 and 1924. He termed these hand-picked replacements "Interventors." A *tenente* from Brazil's impoverished Northeast, João Alberto, moved as São Paulo's Interventor to put the power of the new Ministry of Labor to work in settling the disputes. Even before those strikes, the Interventor declared a 5% across-the-board wage increase and establishment of a 40-hour work week in the factories. He also lowered taxes and fees on industry to help stimulate production in the face of the unfolding economic depression. Alberto and Brazil's first Minister of Labor, Lindolfo Collor, next negotiated settlements between striking textile workers and São Paulo's leading industrialists. With work resuming in the city's factories, Vargas's plans to centralize political and even economic authority in the national capital seemed to have been vindicated. São Paulo's powerful industrial and agriculture elites did not, however, like what they had seen.

As the nation's most powerful state during the Old Republic, São Paulo either made national policy or was left alone to do so without the federal government's interference. Paulista elites saw Vargas's moves to centralize political and even economic policy making in Rio as an existential threat to their power. Their reaction spoke to how dire they considered the situation to be: on July 9, 1932, the state of São Paulo declared a civil war against the federal government.

In under two full months of combat, São Paulo demonstrated that one – albeit quite powerful – state could challenge the federal government's authority and military. Although the Brazilian Army defeated the Paulista Força Pública, the nation's generals noted that had the insurgents had better leadership, they might have defeated the federal government. The 1932 Civil War, as it is known, was hardly the last gasp of state power. Although Vargas won militarily, he dramatically curtailed his plans to centralize power in Rio. Nationally, he tempered his plans. In São Paulo, the nation's most populous and prosperous state, he turned over control of the new Ministry of Labor to the state Department of Labor, which was run by a Paulista industrialist, Jorge Street. The federal government would not reenter the state in a significant way until a massive strike wave in 1953.

Although he limited the federal government's presence in São Paulo, Vargas continued to try to concentrate power in Rio through Brazil's first serious attempts at fashioning national developmentalism. His first major financial commitment was actually geared toward subsidizing Paulista agriculture. During the Depression, Vargas moved to support coffee using the federal government in an unprecedented way. (The Coffee Valorization program during the Old Republic had been financed and run by state governments.) Vargas's coffee support program was the first major Keynesian intervention in the Brazilian economy. The national government created a new permanent government institution and used deficit spending to prop up the coffee sector. Although Vargas had not necessarily intended to do so, the massive infusion of money into São Paulo ended up also supporting the state's industrial economy. Vargas created the National Coffee Council (Conselho Nacional do Café or CNC) in 1931, and so created the first major institution to influence Brazilian economic development from the national capital. That is ironic because nearly 70 years after his death by suicide in 1954, Vargas is remembered more for his role in mobilizing support among the nation's working people.

One of the other key institutions Vargas created in the 1930s to promote national developmentalism was a propaganda ministry based in Rio. The Department of Press and Propaganda (Departamento de Imprensa e Propaganda or DIP) promoted the idea that Vargas's corporatist industrial relations structure promoted social peace and worker productivity through state-sanctioned unions that provided many social services and a series of labor courts to settle wage and other disputes. His ideas were shaped by the pragmatism of wanting to hold on to power. Probably his only closely held political conviction was his belief in his ability to knit together the nation. That impulse became obvious in 1937 when he declared that he would not hold the elections he had promised back in late 1930, and instead Brazil would operate under his New State (Estado Novo) dictatorship.

Vargas had been governing as Brazil's provisional president since he assumed office through the so-called Revolution of 1930 in November of that year. A failed 1935 coup attempt by the Communist Party ordered by the Comintern in Moscow, along with the presence of the openly fascist Integralist movement, gave Vargas the excuse to cancel the elections. He formally declared Brazil to be in the New State dictatorship in a national radio address on November 10, 1937. In a bizarre ceremony to mark the beginning of this new phase of his rule, Vargas stood on stage during a nationally broadcast ceremony which was filmed for newsreels and later shown in cinemas throughout the nation – and spoke directly to the Brazilian flag, pledging allegiance to it, while his attorney general burned each state's flag behind him. The Estado Novo period (1937–45) would accomplish a number of important things, but first and foremost the era was a period of Vargas using dictatorial powers to try to draw the nation together into a coherent whole.

Given the power of the DIP's propaganda, one way the regime emphasized nation building was through the promotion of nationwide unionization and the development of a corporatist industrial relations system. The ideas behind this push fit with Vargas's broad developmentalist goals. The Ministry of Labor would promote social peace and so industrial productivity by managing wage disputes through a tripartite court system with one representative of industry, labor, and the government. (In practice, the deciding vote and so all the power rested with the Ministry of Labor representative.) Moreover, workers were to be organized into unions by industrial category and municipality. Every Brazilian worker paid a mandatory union tax (*imposto sindical*), which was sent to the Ministry of Labor in Rio, and then redistributed to national, state, and local labor federations and unions. The union tax was perhaps the broadest national tax system in the nation's history. For the first time, Brazilian working people in every state and region sent taxes to the national capital. The only national taxes in existence before this were on imports and exports, and so were paid indirectly by some consumers some of the time. The financing of the industrial relations system was Brazil's first coherent national source of personal taxation, and it succeeded in funding important functions of the national government.

The *imposto sindical*'s impact on unionization and workers' rights and pay was much more limited. Union leaders, who had to be approved by the Ministry after an election by members, often chose to keep their organizations small. In order to join, a worker had to be *sindicalizado/a*, which involved gaining the approval of Ministry officials (which was pro forma), and they had to pay dues beyond the union tax. But tax money filtered through the Ministry remained the primary source of funding for these unions. Officials could be reelected by providing a great deal of services to their small membership. A larger union would dilute the budget provided by the *imposto sindical*. Given that all wage and other disputes were handled by the tripartite labor courts, there was no value in having a large membership for public demonstrations and strikes, because they were illegal. Unions also could not be

THE FAILED MARCH TO MODERNITY (1930–1964)

used to mobilize voters at this time because Vargas did not hold any elections. Union density throughout Brazil was, therefore, quite low at this time.

Brazil's economic geography further limited the impact of the national industrial relations system. The regions that most needed the federal government's help to integrate into the national economy and political system had the least industry, and agricultural workers were largely excluded from the Ministry's work. Internal Ministry of Labor documents at this time referred to rest of the nation outside of Rio de Janeiro as "the interior." It had no presence in São Paulo after the 1932 Civil War, and it barely operated outside of the national capital. Vargas therefore used other government programs to attempt to transform the nation. The three that had the most profound impact on Brazil and dramatically altered the role of the federal government were the development of the São Francisco River basin, the so-called March to the West, and the creation of a national steel industry in Volta Redonda.

Work on the São Francisco, which connects the Center-South to the Northeast, and the support for the development of the interior states of Goiás, Matto Grosso do Sul, and Tocantins in the Center-West, and Acre, Amazonas, Amapá, Pará, Rondônia, and Roraima in the North, but often referred to as the Amazon region, were explicit attempts to use the federal government to spur migration from Brazil's coast to the interior. Although these interior spaces had long been occupied by indigenous people, runaway slaves, and others who chose not to be part of Brazilian society, political and economic elites considered them "empty," and so moved to transform them into more integrated parts of the nation. Vargas initiated these programs, and they had only just begun when he was forced out of office in 1945. He did succeed, however, in creating federal bureaucratic mechanisms for these programs, which would continue into the 1970s.

The building of the massive steel complex in Volta Redonda was one of Vargas's most successful programs, and one that highlighted the transformation of Brazil from a coffee exporter to an industrialized economy. In 1942, after pressure from the United States and a series of German submarine attacks on Brazilian shipping, Vargas committed Brazilian troops to the war effort against the Axis powers. There were multiple domestic risks to the move. Brazil was home to the majority of Japanese-heritage people living outside of Japan, and southern Brazil – including Vargas's home state of Rio Grande do Sul – had a sizable German-speaking population. Leadership in the Army was also overwhelmingly pro-German at this time. But the biggest risk Vargas took in joining forces with the Allies was his close association with Franklin Roosevelt and the Allied war aims laid out in 1941's Atlantic Charter. Unlike World War I, World War II was a battle for self-determination and democracy, at least according to FDR and Winston Churchill, whose views on maintaining the British Empire he separated

THE FAILED MARCH TO MODERNITY (1930–1964)   61

from the idea of liberating German- and Japanese-occupied Europe and Asia. Vargas was an awkward fit for the Atlantic Charter's lofty goals. He led an avowedly dictatorial regime during the Estado Novo, and yet he committed Brazil to send troops to Europe to fight against fascism.

Brazil provided naval air stations for the United States, and it guaranteed a steady flow of commodities, such as rubber, bauxite, and coffee. The Army next sent the Brazilian Expeditionary Force to fight under American General Mark Clark in Italy. The Brazilian Army acquired the latest military equipment and the prestige of fighting in Europe. Brazil also received technical support in building its steel industry. The US government then began work on an advanced engine factory in Rio de Janeiro that was to become part of the American military supply chain. The steel facility at Volta Redonda had both an immediate and a long-term impact on Brazil. Its location in the state of Rio, but near the borders of São Paulo and Minas Gerais, was strategic in a number of ways. The military wanted it off the coast to avoid possible naval bombardment. Economic planners wanted it near the burgeoning industrial centers in São Paulo, Minas, and Rio. Those planners were also pleased to use the land of a derelict coffee plantation in the Paraíba Valley, where slave labor had fueled Brazil's first coffee boom in the 1840s. Creating a set of advanced industrial facilities that would provide needed inputs for yet more industry on the site of Brazil's first coffee plantations symbolized the transitions Vargas was trying to make.

The political impact of Brazil's participation in the war in Europe was subtle at first, and then obvious and powerful. Vargas's propaganda machine carefully promoted the war effort. It went so far as to argue that Brazil's political prisons were very different from those in the Axis countries. In order to address popular unease about living in a dictatorship while simultaneously fighting for self-determination in Europe, Vargas created new institutions to make the transition to becoming a democratic leader. He established two political parties as expressions of what he hoped would be a governing coalition. To try to organize working people, Vargas created the Brazilian Labor Party (Partido Trabahista Brasileiro or PTB). He then created a party for the middle class and members of the newly expanded federal bureaucracy, the Social Democratic Party (Partido Social Democrático or PSD). Vargas spent much of 1943 and 1944 trying to build a political coalition for a democratic transition. The contradictions of his long era of rule as a coup leader, provisional president, dictator, and hopeful democrat came to a head as the war in Europe wound down. Once again, the Brazilian military intervened to facilitate the change. Army leadership forced the dictator to leave office on October 29, 1945, and so guaranteed that there would be a presidential election in December of that year.

An Experiment in Democracy

Brazilian politicians had begun scrambling once it became apparent that fighting for democracy abroad, combined with Vargas's long tenure in office, would bring about some sort of change in leadership. In addition to Vargas's PTD and PSD, conservatives from the business community merged with large landowners throughout the country to form the Democratic National Union (União Democrático Nacional or UDN). The remaining leadership of Brazil's Communist Party (Partido Communista Brasileiro or PCB) also worked to put together lists of candidates for the December 1945 elections. Even though it had only been 15 years since Vargas took office, the old Republican Party was now defunct. The personalist nature of Brazilian politics manifested itself just as Vargas was set to leave office. His supporters – no doubt with his approval – created a movement demanding that he remain in charge.

General Eurico Dutra represented Vargas's PSD, while General Eduardo Gomes of the Air Force ran as the UDN, or anti-Vargas, candidate. Dutra won, and Brazil was again technically a democratic nation. During the Old Republic, the politics of the governors involved elections, but the choices were narrowly construed and the franchise was so limited that only a tiny minority of adult Brazilians could vote. While literacy requirements remained an impediment to voting until the implementation of the 1988 Constitution, more

Brazilians participated in national politics in 1945 than had ever before. Although an election between two serving generals without a broad national franchise did not appear to be much different from the politics of the Old Republic, 1945 was markedly different from 1930. Vargas had succeeded in transforming the political system. It was not democratic, but it was much more responsive to popular interests and even demands than at any previous time in the nation's history.

Vargas had hoped to ride a wave of mobilized workers and middle-class Brazilians to remain in office. He had made a populist turn during the war by finally establishing the minimum wage promised in the 1930s, and by shifting the focus of the tripartite labor courts more in favor of working people. The muted popular response to his removal by the military in October 1945 revealed the limits to his program. The entire project of placing workers into a corporatist structure with state-sponsored labor unions had essentially failed. In São Paulo, Brazil's industrial heartland, few workers bothered to join Vargas's unions. The city's largely female textile workers aggressively avoided the male-run union. Of all the workers who paid the mandatory *imposto sindical*, only about 3% bothered to become union members. The largely male metallurgy sector had only around 5% of its eligible workers join. An even greater expression of the failure of Vargas's industrial relations system was the widespread industrial strikes in São Paulo and Rio de Janeiro soon after he left office. The work stoppages were technically illegal and instigated largely by workers who had avoided the unions and formal left groups like the Communist Party. Workers struck once threats of repression and jailing declined with the end of the Estado Novo.

The fecklessness of much of Brazil's labor and left leadership in the years immediately after the Estado Novo was particularly significant given the changes in the political landscape that Vargas had initiated. Although far from a functioning democracy in 1945, Brazil had a form of broad-based or even mass politics. Vargas had ended the "politics of the governors" when he seized power in 1930. He did not fashion a coherent political system to replace that oligarchical structure, but he expanded the state, and used it to promote a notion of Brazilian citizenship that had never before existed for the majority of the nation's people. In the mid-1930s, Vargas's nationalism made him the first leader to be embraced by the nation's Afro-Brazilian community. The São Paulo-based Black Front (Frente Negra) openly supported the dictator's moves to limit employment of immigrant workers in the city's factories. Vargas used radio and newsreels to promote himself as the "Father of the Poor." In response, thousands of Brazil's poor people wrote to Vargas directly criticizing elites and seeking his help in everything from work disputes to neighborhood infrastructure needs. Many of those letters included a proposed deal: if Vargas would give them what they wanted, they would support him.

Vargas's economic program in the 1930–45 period aided both agriculture and industry, but did little for the average person. Real wages dropped as food prices and rents soared during the war years. Those conditions brought on the massive strikes after the repressive machinery of the Estado Novo had been removed. But even though a coalition between the nation's poor and Vargas did not develop, for the first time in Brazil's history, a leader attempted to bring the nation's people into politics. Vargas did not manage to create a viable political coalition, but he did stoke popular interest in politics. That change would accelerate and deepen Brazil's political development. An increasing number of people would pressure a political system that was not designed to respond to popular demands.

The years immediately after Vargas's 1945 ouster revealed the new fragility in the system. The 1945 election elevated a former Army general, Eurico Gaspar Dutra, to the presidency. The 1946 Constitution replaced the illiberal Estado Novo document, but did so in ways that still limited the franchise and kept the national government in control of the industrial relations system. Politically, there were two Brazils. At the top, there was a nominally open system with an elected legislature and president. For the vast majority of Brazilians, however, formal politics was still an elite realm. There were, admittedly, some populist politicians. Indeed, Vargas was using the PTB to position himself as such. The Communist Party, meanwhile, was more active in electoral politics than in labor or peasant organizing. Both Vargas and the Communists often received the support of the working class and poor who had access to the vote (the franchise remained highly circumscribed). Nevertheless, politics for the majority of Brazilians involved activities outside of the electoral system.

Wildcat strikes, bus burnings, and even land seizures in the rural sector were the more common political practices for most Brazilians in the post-Estado Novo period than voting for a candidate who they believed supported their interests. Their actions outside the formal industrial relations and political systems revealed Vargas's complex political legacy. He had dramatically raised popular expectations and invited the majority of Brazilians into the political arena. He did not, however, create the institutions or broader state capacity to meet that dramatic increase in popular demands from the system. Given that imbalance between expectations and the system's capacity to meet them, politics became nearly completely personalistic. No strong parties or other institutions attracted a broad membership. Instead, Brazilians simply supported the politician who spoke to their needs at that moment. Vargas himself recognized this environment when he quickly pivoted and reentered electoral politics for the first time since 1930. In December 1945, he ran for senate seats in both his home state (Rio Grande do Sul) and his adopted home (Rio de Janeiro), winning both and choosing to serve from the former.

The nation's economy had also been dramatically altered by 15 years of Vargas's rule. Brazil and the rest of Latin America benefited from high commodity prices throughout the war and during the rebuilding of Europe through much of the Korean War (1950–3). The problem Brazil faced in this period was that no matter how well the agriculture export sector performed, the nation continued to face a foreign exchange shortfall. Despite the growth of the industrial sector since 1930, the country imported a steadily increasing number of manufactured goods at high prices. The end of the Estado Novo also ended the massive government role in directly supporting various sectors in the economy. Some politicians, especially in the conservative, anti-Vargas UDN, hoped to return to the status quo ante of a laissez-faire system that embraced the nation's comparative advantage as a coffee producer.

Brazil's changing politics and economics dovetailed with a unique moment in world history. Latin American scholars working in Santiago, Chile, were producing a series of critiques of classical liberal economics. They were part of ECLA (Economic Commission for Latin America or CEPAL, Comisión Económica para América Latina in Spanish), a new think tank tied to the United Nations. These economists argued that, as commodity exporters and importers of manufactured goods, Latin American economies were consistently on the losing side of the terms of trade. They eventually labeled the ideas

THE FAILED MARCH TO MODERNITY (1930–1964) **69**

behind this analysis "dependency theory," and argued that the Latin American economies were structured to keep these countries in a state of dependence on the United States and Western Europe.

Before Vargas, most Brazilian politicians would have rejected state action to spur industrialization. Many military leaders, on the other hand, had long embraced some sort of developmentalism since their experiences fighting the Paraguayan War in the 1860s. As founders of the Republic in 1889, they had embraced the slogan "Order and Progress," which adorns the flag to this day, specifically to signal their interest in transforming the nation. Army officers who had gone into the rural sector to put down millenarian uprisings and chase political opponents during the Old Republic were dismayed by Brazil's weak infrastructure and lack of broad economic development. The physical condition and social estrangement from urban Brazilian society also shocked many of these military men. The young officers who initiated the 1922 and 1924 *tenente* uprisings explicitly connected those reactions to the extreme liberalism that defined Brazil as an export economy. They noted that the only real infrastructure existed to facilitate coffee and sugar exports, as well as the importation of foreign-made manufactured goods. In other words, Army officers who started their careers in the 1920s and began to climb the ranks during the Estado Novo were eager by the 1950s and 1960s to embrace many of policy prescriptions the ECLA/

CEPAL economists in Chile were proposing for Latin America.

In the years immediately after the end of World War II, the US government began to promote its own ideas about developmentalism. North American advisors embraced policies that would help Latin American governments break economic bottlenecks, but do little more. In the early 1950s, the Brazilian government welcomed a US mission of economists and other scholars who produced a detailed report filled with recommendations. In 1954, the Joint US-Brazilian commission published *The Development of Brazil*. This built on a program initiated during the Dutra administration (1946–51). After eschewing direct government interventions in the economy, Dutra changed course in 1948 by creating the SALTE (for *Saúde, Alimentação, Transportação, Energia* or Health, Food, Transporation, Energy) plan. This was a five-year schedule for the allocation of key resources. The Joint US–Brazil Commission's report went a bit further by identifying specific bottlenecks that needed to be broken for Brazil's agricultural and industrial sectors to grow. Both of these plans called for public–private partnerships, but with an emphasis on the private sector. Although there was a great deal of energy behind the idea of the government acting, Brazil did not yet have the institutional capacity or political will to accomplish the lofty goals set out by both programs.

The sudden end of the Estado Novo and the December 1945 elections did not magically create

THE FAILED MARCH TO MODERNITY (1930–1964)   71

a new democratic political system. Vargas had succeeded in breaking the oligarchical structure of the polity and economy, but he did not manage to create either the institutions or programs to continue his policies in a non-dictatorial setting. In other words, no one was prepared to govern a democratic Brazil and use the national government to shape economic policy. The Dutra administration was largely successful in that it benefited from the large foreign reserves earned during the war, and as Europe rebuilt with massive US aid. Dutra also presided over the writing of a new constitution and he held open national elections for his successor. While having those elections was a reassuring sign of political progress, the franchise remained highly circumscribed (illiterate people could not vote, and the weak educational system did little to increase literacy in Brazil). The results of the 1950 presidential election revealed just how limited that progress was.

Getúlio Vargas handily won with just under 49% of the vote. He ran as the candidate of the Brazilian Labor Party (PTB), and defeated Eduardo Gomes (the former military man who had run against Dutra in 1945) from the conservative UDN and Cristiano Machado who ran under the PSD, which Vargas had founded at the same time as he created the PTB. These party affiliations were of little importance, though. As noted above, politics was personalistic, and the Brazilian electorate wanted a known quantity. Vargas had governed Brazil for 15 years from 1930 to 1945 at first as a provisional president with few checks on his authority, and then as an outright dictator with access to a powerful state propaganda machine. Even during the Estado Novo dictatorship, he was still a politician who had to juggle a wide variety of interest groups, but doing that without meaningful popular or elite opposition hardly prepared him to act in an open political system with vocal adversaries and a free press. Vargas tried to balance the interests of capital and labor by implementing many of the suggestions of the Joint Report while also loosening the federal government's control over unions. He did not increase regulations on business. Instead, he used the federal government to begin to break various bottlenecks holding back the Brazilian economy. By creating a national oil company, Petrobras, he sought to provide steady and less expensive access to energy, while at the same time he could stoke broad nationalist pride by laying claim to some initial petroleum discoveries. Vargas proudly proclaimed that "The oil is ours" ("*o petroleo é nosso*").

Vargas also created the National Bank for Economic Development (Banco Nacional de Desenvolvimento Econômico e Social or BNDES) in 1952, which, along with Petrobras (which was formally established in 1953), completed the move away from the extreme economic liberalism of the Old Republic. Brazil now had institutions created in an open political system that placed the federal government in the forefront of the sort of developmentalism some intellectuals, businessmen, and military leaders had been discussing since the late nineteenth century. What distinguished Petrobras and the BNDES from Vargas's previous state making in the 1930–45 period was the fact that these new institutions had broad popular support and had been created in a democratic milieu.

Despite these successes, Vargas had trouble operating in an open political environment. He faced opponents on the left and right, and he could not always manage to keep members of his political coalition in line. While the Communist Party openly opposed him, workers without ties to political parties or movements launched devastatingly effective strikes. In 1953, a broad coalition of São Paulo city factory workers demanded significant wage increases. The so-called Strike of the 300,000 (out of a total population of around 1.2 million people) lasted five weeks and resulted in double-digit wage gains. Even with this success, however, the city's working people recognized that their wage demands were based on inflation numbers and other statistics produced by government agencies they did not trust. As a result, they developed their own Inter-Union Department of Statistics and Socio-Economic Studies (Departamento Intersindical de Estatíticas e Estudos Sócio-Econômicos or DIEESE) to gather wage and cost of living data independent of the federal Ministry of Labor. Although no one at the time realized it, DIEESE's creation would fundamentally alter the balance of power between rank-and-file workers and the state for decades to come. In the short term, it was an important reminder of the incomplete nature of Vargas's state making. The Ministry of Labor had the tools necessary to manage industrial relations in a formal sense, especially during periods of dictatorship when challenging its decisions had significant costs. But it did not have either the institutional capacity or confidence of the broad population to operate as a trusted actor in Brazil's industrial disputes.

The president tried to placate the nation's working people by making a young, progressive politician from his home state of Rio Grande do Sul, João "Jango" Goulart, the new Labor Minister after the massive 1953 strike. Goulart recommended doubling the national minimum wage, which had not been raised since 1951, and never reached a livable level (the minimum wage was set so low that the salaries of the nation's poor were expressed as multiple minimum wages, e.g. day laborers "earned three minimum wages"). This plan brought immediate condemnation from the business community. Goulart next proposed extending unionization to agricultural workers, enraging Brazil's planters.

The political right, as represented by the UDN, tried and failed to use legislative tactics to remove Vargas. They loudly denounced him and his government. After so many years of witnessing an expanding national government, conservatives complained about federal spending and the national debt. They also decried any hint of personal corruption among

Vargas's political allies. Segments of the military's leadership moved toward removing the president. Brazil's military had played a central role in a number of major political transitions, most significantly in 1889 with the fall of the Empire, the Revolution of 1930, and Vargas's 1945 ouster. Once again, leading officers began to consider their options as Vargas seemingly lost control of Brazilian politics.

A far-right journalist, Carlos Lacerda, who had begun his political life in the 1930s as a Communist, led the charge against Vargas through a newspaper he controlled. Lacerda openly plotted with fellow UDN politicians and sympathetic military officers. His opposition was relentless, so when a Vargas ally, probably acting on his own, attempted to assassinate Lacerda, Vargas's hold on power waned. The president famously said of the corruption and political intrigue surrounding him, "I feel I am standing in a sea of mud." On the evening of August 24, 1954, Vargas extricated himself from this political morass. He wrote out a lengthy note, and then killed himself with a revolver in the bedroom of the Presidential Palace in Rio. His suicide note spoke of his enemies as the enemies of the people: "Once more the forces and interests against the people are newly coordinated and raised against me." His message to the nation invokes themes of nationalism and national development. Vargas then continues by placing himself at the center of Brazil's past and future: "I gave you my life. Now I offer you my death. Nothing remains. Serenely,

I take my first step on the road to eternity, and I leave life to enter history."

Shock and anger were the initial reactions among Vargas's supporters, but after a few weeks of sporadic protests and marches, the political environment calmed. The military did not seize power, and Brazil followed the constitutional order by elevating Vice President João Café Filho to the presidency. That smooth transition did not last long. Café Filho, as most Brazilians knew at the time, was an opponent of most of Vargas's economic policies. Brazilian presidential elections did not necessarily include unified party tickets: in 1950, Vargas and Café Filho had won the presidency and vice presidency from different parties (respectively the PTB and the Social Progressive Party: Partido Social Progressista or PSP), and they had different political agendas. (The absence of unified presidential tickets would dramatically affect Brazilian politics in 1961 and again in 2016.) The new president restructured the cabinet and installed well-known anti-Vargas politicians. Café Filho's primary policy differences with Vargas centered on the state's role in promoting industrialization and building infrastructure. The new president had a conservative view of the state, and so appointed a UDN politician as the new Finance Minister. He was even urged to postpone the October congressional elections because his allies feared Vargas's suicide would engender popular support for PTB candidates. The elections were held as scheduled, but Vargas's PTB did not make significant gains, demonstrating again that Brazilian politics remained more tied to personalities than institutions. With Vargas gone from the political scene, there was no clear favorite pro- or anti-Vargas candidate for the 1955 presidential elections.

The coming election again highlighted the flimsiness of Brazil's political parties. Beginning with the Revolution of 1930, and deepening with the declaration of the explicitly dictatorial Estado Novo in 1937, the nation's politics became largely binary. People with an opinion either supported Vargas or defined themselves in opposition to him and the federal government's expanding role in the economy, especially the promotion of industry. At first, it seemed as though the presidential candidates would take on little more than pro- and anti-Vargas stances. The conservative UDN explicitly ran against his legacy, and the party chose an interesting candidate to do that: General Juarez Távora. He had been an important leader of the *tenente* movement and a supporter of the Revolution of 1930. He broke with Vargas in 1937, and then became a leader in intellectual military circles, and was a Café Filho ally who entered the administration after Vargas's suicide.

"Fifty Years of Progress in Five" and Three Years of Chaos

Pro-Vargas forces took back control of the PSD and nominated Juscelino Kubitschek, the popular governor of Minas Gerais. JK, as he was known, ran on an arranged ticket with Vargas's former Labor Minister, João "Jango" Goulart, who carried the mantle of the PTB. The duo walked a fine line between mobilizing Vargas's supporters and attracting new support. Jango, who was from Vargas's home town of São Borja in Rio Grande do Sul and was closely associated with the previous administration, was only 37 years old in 1955 and so came to represent a new generation of politician. He was also much more closely tied to the populist aspects of Vargas's administration, having been the first truly pro-worker Minister of Labor in the history of that position.

Kubitschek, although in some ways connected to Vargas, was very much his own man. The son of a central European immigrant mother whose name he took, JK started his professional life as a public health doctor and worked as a urologist. He went on to be a popular mayor of Belo Horizonte, the Mineiro capital, before being elected the governor of the state. He shaped his presidential campaign around themes of progress, movement, and energy. He proposed a series of major government initiatives to transform the nation and propel it forward. After receiving more votes than any candidate for office in Brazilian history (and with Goulart as his vice president), he convened his cabinet in the early morning hours of his first day in office to finalize his plans for Brazil's ongoing economic and social development. He had promised to provide "fifty years of progress in five" (the length of his term), and he began by issuing his Targets Plan to accomplish that during his presidency.

Kubitschek announced 30 numbered targets in five sectors (Energy, Transportation, Food, Basic Industries, and Education). There was also a "Synthesis Target," which was the building of a new interior capital city, Brasília. He largely succeeded in meeting these targets. During JK's tenure, Brazil dramatically increased the production of industrial inputs, built roads, established the automobile industry with the help of multinational corporations, and even opened Brasília. The material progress during his administration was extraordinary. Culturally and politically, JK demonstrated that Brazilians could accomplish big things through the work of the national government, and they could do so in a democratic setting. The five years that Kubitschek led the nation were, in many ways, among the most significant in Brazil's history since its independence from Portugal in 1822.

From Vargas's ouster in 1945 until JK's election in 1955, the Brazilian polity and economy were chaotic. Kubitschek seemed to have ushered in a period of political stability and economic growth based on a mix of increased industrial and agricultural output. The 1960 presidential election was seen, at the time, as yet another milestone in Brazil's evolution. Jânio Quadros, a reformer who promised to end the corruption that had accompanied the government's ever-expanding role in the economy, easily won the election with 48.26% of the vote in a three-candidate race. Quadros ran under the banner of three parties, his own party (PTN, Partido Trabalhista Nacional or National Labor Party), a center-right party (PDC, Partido Democrata Cristão or Christian Democratic Party), and the stalwart conservative UDN. He ran against Henrique Teixeira Lott, who had campaigned unsuccessfully in 1945 against Dutra. Lott was the candidate for Vargas's two parties, the PSD and PTB, and he received 32.94% of the vote. The former governor of São Paulo, Adhemar de Barros, who ran under the banner of the Social Progressive Party, which he had founded in the mid-1940s, gained 18.8% of the vote. João "Jango" Goulart, JK's vice president, won another term in that office running as the PSD–PTB candidate.

The positive news about 1960 was that there was a smooth election and transition to a new administration. But the elections also highlighted the ongoing personalism of Brazilian politics. Quadros's campaign promised reform. He used a broom as his symbol for how he would clean up Brazilian politics. He also embraced a nationalism that sought to distance Brazil slightly from the United States by having full diplomatic relations with both China and Cuba. But there was not much more to his platform than that. He was elected as the young outsider, as opposed to Lott and Barros, who had been in national politics since the 1940s. And Jango, who was the vice president of the very administration Quadros had critiqued as corrupt, was again elected vice president.

As president, Quadros sought to bring down inflation, and to chart a more independent path for Brazil in foreign relations. He immediately reoriented the nation on the world stage by sending a trade mission to China, increasing ties with the Soviet Union, and expanding the country's presence in Africa. He even awarded Ché Guevara the highest honor available to a foreigner, the Order of the Southern Cross. Quadros had visited Cuba during the campaign to signal his distance from many of the conservatives in the UDN. Foreign affairs were easy. Making changes domestically was much more challenging given how Quadros's room to maneuver was severely limited by the way the Constitution of 1946 structured Brazilian politics. The biggest and richest states' urban areas largely elected the president through a direct vote. São Paulo, Minas Gerais, and the state of Rio de Janeiro accounted for more than half of the votes for president. But Brazil's vast rural areas shaped the Congress. Rural bosses (the *coronéis*) still controlled the vote in the countryside, and so determined the fate of the Brazilian Senate. The richest four states produced a quarter of the number of senators that the poorer states sent to Brasília.

Quadros fought with the Congress over almost every aspect of his domestic agenda. He sought constitutional reform, but even his allies from the wealthier states were loath to support him given how he had lurched foreign policy to the left in the aftermath of the 1959 Cuban Revolution. The president knew he had to do something dramatic, and so he leveraged conservatives' dislike and fear of his vice president, João Goulart, when he acted. After a mere seven months in office, Quadros attempted to gain increased presidential authority by threatening to resign and leave Brazil with Jango as president. Politicians from across the political spectrum called his bluff, and Quadros ended up resigning the presidency on August 25, 1961.

While most Brazilians were angry with Quadros, they were divided over what would come next. Jango happened to be in China on a trade mission when he was unexpectedly elevated to the presidency. A number of conservative military men argued publicly against allowing him to assume that office. Those generals' opposition horrified many Brazilians, who increasingly saw their nation as a democracy. The generals' plans to stop the transition ironically guaranteed Goulart would ascend to the presidency, albeit under unique circumstances. Jango had to negotiate the contours of his presidential authority with his political opponents. He ended up agreeing to the temporary establishment of a quasi-parliamentary system that gave the conservative, rural-based legislature equal power with the president. A quickly crafted constitutional amendment created a Council of Ministers to share power. This mollified some in the military, and gave moderates and others a sense that the constitutional order had held.

Jango had a lot of political goodwill from Brazilians because he was embraced as the individual who best represented and protected the nation's nascent democracy. Unfortunately for him and Brazil, he quickly squandered that broad support. Conservatives read him as being too radical and tied to labor. Many on the left saw him as part of Vargas's legacy of government control of or even manipulation of working people. Goulart responded by addressing issues that could have broad appeal. He created a national electric utility, Electrobras, to expand energy production and distribution. And he moved to try to keep a larger share of foreign corporations' profits from leaving Brazil, which had been repatriated at high rates. That move ended up limiting new foreign investment in the country at the same time that public debt continued to balloon in the wake of JK's massive spending. Inflation followed, which only deepened people's sense of economic chaos. Rather than work to reduce inflation or at least mitigate its impact on the nation's poor, Goulart claimed it was nothing more than a symptom of Brazil healthy and growing economy.

With popular pressure mounting, Jango argued that he could not fix Brazil's economy without the return of full presidential powers. In a plebiscite on January 6, 1963, 12 million Brazilians (out of a population of 43 million people of voting age) voted on the matter. By a five to one margin, voters called for Jango to have full presidential authority. Although the political wind was at his back, however, Goulart faced a daunting list of problems. Inflation remained high, while urban labor and landless peasants were agitating for relief. The Congress largely opposed his administration, as did growing numbers of military men and the US government. Jango responded by proposing a desperately needed agrarian reform. Although long overdue as policy, it was both a long-term solution in the face of current problems and one that required a two-thirds vote in the Congress because it would need to be a constitutional amendment to take effect. The proposal failed, and Brazil increasingly split between a left seeking deep reforms and conservatives who invoked the Cuban Revolution as a way of demonizing those calls for significant change.

Jango decided to put a broad range of reforms into something he called the Package Plan in February 1964. Illiterate people were to receive the right to vote, non-commissioned officers were to be given full political rights, and the Communist Party would be legalized. There were also broad changes in the tax code, indexing of wages, new state monopolies over the export of coffee, iron ore, and other commodities, and new mining concessions. The Package Plan attempted to redistribute land around federal highways, railroads, and water projects as a nascent agrarian reform. Then in March, rural workers struck seeking labor regulations for the agricultural sector. On March 13, about 150,000 people attended an event at which the president signed his modest agrarian reform. His political allies openly called to ignore the Congress. A few days later, Jango extended voting rights to illiterate people and non-commissioned officers without legislative approval.

Conservatives organized public protests, including the so-called March of the Family with God for Liberty in São Paulo on March 19. Behind the scenes, the US government sent officers who had served with Brazilians in Europe during World War II to encourage action. Lyndon Johnson's administration also offered covert aid to the Brazilian military if they moved against the president. Brazil's generals remained divided over how to proceed but then, on March 30, 1964, the president spoke at a meeting of the Military Police Sergeants Association and openly criticized Brazil's generals and admirals, claiming they lacked discipline. The coup began the next day. Troops converged on Rio, where much of Brazil's political leadership was still concentrated. Jango first fled to Brasília, and then to his home state of Rio Grande do Sul, and finally across the border to Uruguay. With that, the Brazilian experiment in democracy ended. Although few realized it at the time, Brazil was beginning a two-decade dictatorship during which the country's military claimed it would fulfill its historic mission to transform the nation economically, socially, and politically.

3
Military Dictatorship (1964–1985)

When tanks filled the streets of Rio de Janeiro on April 1, 1964, they signaled two important moments in Brazilian history: they ended the nation's brief experiment with electoral politics; and they fulfilled the goals of a segment of the military that stretched back to the institution's founding during the Paraguayan War in the 1860s. In the most immediate sense, the military ended the political chaos of the moment. Upon taking control, the generals promised to practice "the politics of anti-politics." They claimed that they would do whatever it took to promote Brazilian economic growth and development, whether it was politically popular or not. They said they would be technocrats. Those promises were based in their long-held self-image as Brazil's only reliable, powerful, and cohesive national institution.

Over their course of two decades of rule, Brazil's military leaders tried to put into practice policies that would transform the nation and make it worthy of the military itself. They did so through an explicitly authoritarian framework, but one that allowed for varying degrees of popular pushback, and even limited elections for some national, state, and local offices. The generals began their rule in the mid-1960s believing they could run the nation indefinitely. By the late 1970s, they were working tirelessly to engineer a peaceful exit from power that would preclude the establishment of truth commissions and trials for their extensive human rights violations.

There were several features of this 21-year military dictatorship that distinguished it from others in Latin America during roughly the same period. In addition to the maintenance of some elections, the Brazilian military made sure that they could argue that they were acting legally. The generals issued a series of so-called Institutional Acts to serve as the legal framework for their actions. They did this not only to establish a sense of legitimacy, but also because Brazil had a long tradition of making declarations of legality to fit a desired outcome. In 1840, when leaders of the Regency made then-14-year-old Pedro II an 18-year-old adult with a simple pronouncement, they established this Brazilian sense of legitimacy. The military also acted in this way during its long era of rule in order to maintain institutional cohesion and integrity. And after a decade in power when some leading generals began to worry about the military's ongoing cohesion as a leading national institution, it began the process of returning Brazil to civilian rule.

The Military in Power

In its first few months of rule, the military focused on calming the chaos of the Quadros and Goulart years. Installing a general as president and destroying the constitutional order did little to ease tensions, however. Those moves unnerved Brazilians across the political spectrum. The military had directly governed Brazil once before. After ousting Pedro II and bringing the Empire to an end, the Army took control of the nascent Republic. The military's Deodoro de Fonseca and Floriano Peixoto ruled from 1889 to 1894, when civilian politicians assumed power. The military remained a key player in Brazilian politics, however. It installed, supported, and later removed Getúlio Vargas in the 1930 to 1945 period. Military men also openly influenced politics, and even helped to set the terms of João Goulart's ascension from the vice presidency to the presidency in 1961. Many in Brazil expected a similar brief intervention in 1964. Conservative politicians in the UDN, particularly its most vocal leader, Carlos Lacerda, thought the military would cleanse the political system of radicals and populists, and then turn over power to its civilian allies, like Lacerda himself.

Under the leadership of General Humberto Castelo Branco, the military removed many civilian politicians from the system. Although it brutally repressed workers, union leaders, and left activists in major metropolitan areas and peasant league leaders in the Northeast, it used a unique Brazilian tool to silence elite opponents in the political system. It made them "*cassado/a.*" Once made *cassado/a*, someone was forbidden from speaking publicly about political matters.

This move signaled three aspects of the developing military dictatorship. First, there would be some, albeit highly circumscribed, political debates. Second, it also pointed to the continued class nature of repression in Brazil. Workers, unionists, and peasants faced violence at the hands of the military, while politicians, who were upper-middle class or wealthy, were merely ordered to be silent on political matters. (As we will see below, the military eroded this distinction later in the decade when even members of the elite faced torture and imprisonment.) And, finally, removing the political rights of regime opponents indicated that the military would indeed govern Brazil going forward. General Castelo Branco transformed himself into President Castelo Branco.

As president, Castelo Branco turned his attention to stabilizing the economy by trying to bring inflation under control. Although it was not yet described as such, the military applied a neoliberal-style shock to the Brazilian economy. The generals running Brazil promised to act as technocrats who would determine the best course of action for the nation, and execute it without regard to the political costs. This was how the "politics of anti-politics" was supposed to work in practice. The regime embraced a number of economists and others who would implement their program. None was more prominent than Roberto Campos, whose policies succeeded in bringing down inflation through a severe economic contraction. Over the course of 1966 and 1967, thousands of

Brazilian-owned businesses filed for bankruptcy, and political instability returned. Multinational corporations, on the other hand, expanded their presence. To many, the military government's policies were denationalizing the economy at the expense of the average Brazilian.

The public responded with broad-based popular protests over the course of 1968. Although their actions were not obviously coordinated, industrial workers, university students, and others openly protested against the regime's policies. The presence of students was the first warning sign for the regime. University student politics had not previously taken such a radical or anti-status quo stance. The fact that the children of the upper-middle class and elite were turning against the military dictatorship was destabilizing for the generals, who had predicated their seizure of power on the idea of them representing the best hope for the nation. When thousands of Brazilian business leaders joined in opposing regime policies, the military government faced its first real crisis of legitimacy.

General Artur Costa e Silva followed Castelo Branco into the presidency in 1967, and he turned his attention to quelling popular unrest. He served for about two and half years before stepping aside in October 1969 after suffering a stroke. His brief tenure, though, revealed a great deal about how the military dictatorship would operate. Costa e Silva, like his predecessor, removed his uniform. He appeared in public in a regular suit and tie and he was referred to as "president" rather than "general." That was more than a simple linguistic ploy. The military men and their civilian allies made the transition to politicians, and even joined a new party, the National Renewal Alliance or ARENA (Aliança Renovadora Nacional). They started to define the "politics of anti-politics" as operating within a highly circumscribed political system. There would be some press freedom, but not too much. There were to be elections, but often with elaborate rules meant to tilt the vote toward the pro-regime party.

Making sure to always act "legally," the military issued Institutional Act Number 2 during the Castelo Branco administration. It closed the pre-coup political parties and called for the creation of two new ones: the pro-regime ARENA and the opposition grouped into the Brazilian Democratic Movement or MDB (Movimento Democrático Brasilierio). Although never stated, these changes highlighted not an anti-politics, but a controlled system. The choice of a two-party system had some obvious advantages. The generals spoke of the appeal of the British and North American two-party tradition, but there was more to it. First, it administratively and legally – although not in practice – ended the Communist Party. The change also allowed the military to rely on its own party, and not the UDN, which was not popular among large segments of the electorate. Next, it created a sense of order, which was always important to the military. Elections would no longer be about personalities, complex coalitions, and parties that came and went. The vote would be a simple binary choice between the regime and its opponents.

The military could use Institutional Acts and other tools to make sure the electorate tilted toward ARENA candidates and away from those in the MDB. And to maintain their grip on power, the generals inserted into Institutional Act Number 2 the indirect election of the president through a congressional vote. Institutional Act Number 3 added a similar indirect election of state governors through their legislatures. Those governors were also empowered to appoint the state capitals' mayors. The clearest power grab in the Act was the prohibition on judicial reviews of this and other Institutional Acts. The next one (Number 4) terminated the constitution, which had been in place since 1946, and collected the previous decrees into a new governing document.

Even with all of these authoritarian structures in place, the regime did not control the situation on the ground. The aforementioned strikes in 1968 demonstrated the limits of military governance. The politics of anti-politics was little more than an excuse for the dictatorship. The regime allowed for extra-legal labor negotiations when the first workers struck in April 1968, but then changed course and embraced the old corporatist framework Vargas had created to channel industrial relations through the state. The military regime cracked down on all protests. University students who protested in 1968 were overwhelmingly middle and upper-middle class. Throughout its history, Brazilian governments had violently suppressed slaves, peasants, workers, and other non-elite groups. This violence against students revealed the true nature of the regime.

The Hardliners Take Over

Although weak and quixotic, armed rural and urban resistance groups grew and rattled the regime, particularly after the kidnapping of the US Ambassador in September 1969. Kidnappings were used to undermine popular faith in the government and to demand prisoner releases. Whatever small successes these guerrilla movements had with their short-term demands, their actions only deepened the resolve of the most conservative members of the military and their civilian allies to repress dissent expressed outside the highly circumscribed formal political system.

The generals had no interest in creating a totalitarian state. They sought to act as guardians of the economy, not its master. They also used the Institutional Acts to try to practice a highly circumscribed form of electoral politics. But when new laws and structures failed to contain popular unrest, the generals turned to violence. Violence against real and perceived political opponents became a feature of the regime after the so-called coup within a coup when hardline officers took control with the elevation of General Emílio Garrastazu Médici to the presidency in 1969. The regime under Médici (1969–74) functioned as bureaucratic authoritarianism, in that the military and its technocrat allies governed Brazil through laws, decrees, and violence. Although Médici presided over a period of increased violence against the broad population, however, it was the result of the rise of the hardliners within the ranks of the military, and not just the whims of one general.

That distinction mattered. Brazilian politics had long been dominated by individual leaders rather than parties and movements, especially since Getúlio Vargas embraced broad or mass politics beginning in 1930. The generals were firmly opposed to the idea that any one of them could become what the political scientist Juan Linz referred to a "sultanistic dictator." And despite the myriad problems created by military rule, the focus on bureaucratic leadership had some distinct advantages that manifested themselves during the Médici years, which witnessed unprecedented economic growth.

Brazil's "Economic Miracle" from 1969 to 1973 was a period of annual gross domestic product (GDP) growth of almost 11%. There were some obvious reasons for this prodigious output. It represented, more than anything else, the recovery from the severe recession the military had engineered soon after coming to power in order to bring inflation under control. The widespread strikes and bankruptcies in 1968 had demonstrated the hardships created by that downturn. No one then knew that the economy was on the verge of such a spectacular rebound, even though plenty of other factors signaled its coming. The repressive regime was holding down wages through real and threatened violence against workers and peasants. Moreover, the regime had quietly pivoted from its embrace of laissez-faire policies, and began to play an increasingly activist role in the economy.

An initial reason for 1964's seizure of power was to turn back the clock in terms of economic policy making. Castelo Branco and other military men looked to classical liberal economics and technocrats who promised to implement them. The civilian economist Roberto Campos, who directed much of the regime's policies, was so eager to break down trading barriers with the United States and the United Kingdom that his critics openly anglicized his name and referred to him simply as "Bobby Fields." This extreme embrace of free trade and other traditional liberal economic policies – which a decade later would increasingly be referred to as "neoliberalism" – was at odds with a number of the military's long-held goals, as well as its obvious nationalism. Since the late nineteenth century, the military as an institution had supported a broad developmentalist program for the nation. The generals promoted building infrastructure, and were nominally in favor of programs to elevate the populace socially. As in most militaries, the Brazilian high command was also highly nationalistic, and so feared for patriotic and strategic reasons the impact of the extreme economic liberalism that left the country as an exporter of agricultural commodities and importer of manufactured goods.

Military men had toppled the Empire in 1889, and then helped bring down the Republic in 1930, in part to promote their developmentalist goals. Many of the *tenentes* who had rebelled against the Republic in 1922 and 1924 became key architects of Vargas's Estado Novo, with its extensive interventions in the economy. It was not, therefore, surprising when the hardliners around Médici changed course and began to insert the state more forcefully in the national economy. They created numerous new state institutions to coordinate investments throughout Brazil among domestic businesses, foreign capital and corporations, and the federal government. During the years of the Economic Miracle, the regime quickly took credit for the record levels of growth. Although the benefits of that expansion were concentrated at the top of the social structure, the boom was so robust that nearly everyone's economic circumstances improved to some extent. The national mood was further buoyed by Brazil's World Cup victory in 1970, its third in the last four tournaments (the team won the 1958 and 1962 games; England won in 1966).

That optimism was bolstered by Brazilians again looking to the future with a series of massive, state-run developmentalist projects. The military government in 1970 initiated programs that sought to propel Brazil forward through the transformation of the nation's geography and natural resources. Work on the massive Itaipú Dam on the Paraná River between Brazil and Paraguay began in 1970, although it was not completed until 1984. Its power plant is so massive that it produces electricity for both São Paulo and Rio de Janeiro, which is almost 1,500 km from the dam. At the same time, the military government also began to implement its National Integration Program or PIN (Programa de Integração Nacional), which called for the construction of a series of roads and highways far into the nation's interior, especially the North. Work began on the 4,000-km Trans-Amazonian Highway (known in the nation as BR 230), which runs through seven of Brazil's largest states, in 1972. BR 230 was part of an ambitious state-led program to transform Amazonia into a well-populated and agriculturally productive region. The generals hoped to diminish the growing population density of the nation's largest cities by encouraging migration to the North, and they looked at the area as a great untapped resource for national development. The program succeeded in transforming much of the region, but often through destructive and extensive deforestation.

At the end of Médici's five-year term in 1974, General Ernesto Geisel took control of Brazil. Although another military dictator serving as president, Geisel was in many ways the ultimate technocrat. He successfully navigated new economic challenges, and even initiated discussions on how the military could eventually peacefully leave power and reestablish civilian governance. He first had to deal with two crises, however. One was obvious and the other simmering under the surface.

Geisel's first task was to deal with the unwinding of Brazil's Economic Miracle in the face of crushing petroleum prices and mounting public debt. Part of the developmentalism the military had long espoused focused on the physical transformation of the nation. Brazil is Latin America's geographically largest nation, but it had not created an effective infrastructure connecting its far-flung regions. For most of its colonial and early national history, the country relied on coastal sea travel and mule trains to move people and goods. Foreign capital financed rail construction beginning in the mid-nineteenth century, but it focused more on the movement of commodities from the interior to the coast than on creating lines of communications among the states. People dreamed that air travel might tie the nation together, but it proved to be an expensive and impractical option. Still, Brazilians were so enamored of the idea of flight as a key to national unification that the outline of Brasília's city limits is literally in the shape of a plane. At the end of the day, though, Brazil turned to automobiles – trucks, buses, and personal cars – to link the nation.

The push to transform and connect the nation through automobility began tentatively under Vargas, but was accelerated by Kubitschek when he used the federal government to build highways throughout the nation, and then brought in multinational corporations to build autos of all sorts in Brazil. Reliance on trucks, buses, and cars grew steadily, and then personal car ownership increased dramatically during the Economic Miracle. Brazil, in turn, steadily raised its petroleum imports from the 1930s onward. The oil discoveries celebrated by Vargas when he created Petrobras in 1953 turned out to be illusory. By the time of the 1970s oil shocks, Brazil had no choice but to increase its massive debt to pay the growing bill. Higher energy prices combined with the cost of debt service undermined the economy's health.

Geisel responded by continuing to support oil imports in the short term, and then also investing heavily in alternative energy. The government's National Ethanol Program (Proálcool) was a near perfect example of the regime's ideology and practice. The military, which had come to power espousing laissez-faire tropes about the virtues of the free market and the dangers of government overreach, inserted itself into multiple sectors of the Brazilian economy. The National Ethanol Program provided a major lifeline to the nation's languishing sugar sector. The regime invested heavily in modern refineries near sugar plantations in São Paulo and various states in the Northeast. It also built pipelines to transport the fuel to urban markets and it mandated that the foreign auto companies build ethanol-powered car engines (trucks and buses continued to use diesel fuel). Brazilian passenger vehicles would use a 100% ethanol fuel, as opposed to the standard 90–10% gas-to-ethanol mix found in many countries.

The program had a mixed record. It succeeded in radically reorienting Brazil's energy market, and so did decrease petroleum imports. But it did so at great cost. Ethanol was expensive, and highly subsidized by the national government. And, paradoxically, this plant-based alternative fuel was an environmental disaster as sugar producers ramped up production in dangerous ways that degraded the soil and water in and around their fields. The costs to the government and environment were long-term problems. In the near term, however, Geisel's administration had successfully addressed a serious problem with aggressive state intervention in the agrarian and industrial economies. Like the building of Brasília during the Kubitschek years, the creation of Proálcool proved the efficacy of the national government in transforming Brazil.

Democracy on the Agenda

Another major transformation was taking place at the same time. The military regime did not plan it or even want it, but the dictatorship was the ultimate cause of the rise of a series of New Social Movements that would change Brazilian politics over the coming decades. Unlike the worker and student strikes in 1968, these new groups were simultaneously reacting against regime policies and creating a new politics beyond the formal dictatorial system. New unions that increasingly rejected the formal, corporatist industrial relations system were the most obvious and successful of these new actors.

Beginning in the 1930s, workers were directly tied to the state. As we saw in the previous chapter, their unions were de facto government institutions. Membership had to be approved by the Ministry of Labor, strikes were illegal, and wage and work disputes were routed to tripartite labor courts made up of one industry representative, one from the unions, and another from the Ministry of Labor. This arrangement vested all the power in the Ministry representative, given the tendency of the industry and labor votes to cancel each other out. Throughout the Vargas years, this corporatist system succeeded in limiting popular organizing and strikes, but also failed to bring workers into the state. Few industrial workers bothered joining the corporatist unions. There were barely any advantages to membership, and union leaders often preferred they not join. Union budgets were determined by the total number of workers in an industrial category in their city or town. A small membership meant union leaders could lavish larger benefits on their rank-and-file, and so easily gain reelection.

Once the dictatorial Estado Novo ended in 1945, workers outside of the formal union structure launched wildcat strikes demanding dramatic wage increases after years of being squeezed by both wartime inflation and the Ministry of Labor. When Vargas returned to the presidency in 1951, he tried to court workers, and so the Ministry largely turned a blind eye to a series of union insurgencies, particularly in the city of São Paulo. Those workers initiated one of the largest and most successful popular actions in Brazilian history. Over the course of five weeks starting in March 1953, more than 300,000 workers in the city, whose population was about 1.2 million people, successfully struck for significant wage increases.

Despite getting significant concessions, the strike leaders understood that their wage demands had been based on official inflation statistics generated by the federal government. After the strike, leaders from the striking industries (textiles, metalworker, glass, and furniture workers) approached the bank workers to create a new group to gather and publish wage and cost of living data. The Inter-Union Department of Statistics and Socio-Economic Studies (DIEESE) started collecting data door-to-door in the mid-1950s, and continued its work throughout democracy and dictatorship. It grew and added economists to its staff but was never prominent enough to generate regime scrutiny, until its inflation data were embraced by foreign banks and government agencies, which in turn rejected the Geisel administration's numbers.

In 1973, the government claimed that Brazil had an inflation rate of about 15%. DIEESE's statistics showed inflation of somewhere in the 20–25% range. In mid-1977, World Bank economists reviewed all the data to try to evaluate inflation over the last few years. They determined that inflation in 1973 had been 22.5%, which was in the exact middle of DIEESE's range and far above the government's number. The World Bank, hardly a tool of radical labor insurgency, chided the Brazilian government and sided with the workers' statistical agency, giving added legitimacy to the growing labor movement in São Paulo's industrial suburbs among workers in the multinational automobile sector. The young metalworkers who became the leaders of the New Unionism movement in Brazil were careful to cultivate approval throughout Brazil and abroad. They situated themselves as completely new actors with no ties to either populist or communist political and labor leaders.

These workers were not alone in presenting new challenges to the regime. The military's use of torture led some in the Catholic Church's hierarchy to move from centrist or even center-right politics to outright opposition to the dictatorship. São Paulo's Cardinal Paulo Evaristo Arns connected the rising, progressive Church associated with Liberation Theology, which called for the hierarchy and parish priests to identify with and work on behalf of the poor, with the older, more traditional hierarchy. Although there were other prominent progressive theologians in Brazil and even within the Church hierarchy, such as Dom Hélder Câmara, the Archbishop of Olinda and Recife in the Northeast, Arns was the most powerful and public force opposing the regime's clear excesses, especially its human rights abuses. He had helped to organize a clandestine group that interviewed torture survivors. He made copies of the massive collected record, and sent them abroad for safekeeping. A small book, *Brasil Nunca Mais* (*Brazil Never Again*), was later published in Brazil. A translated version was published in the United States as *Torture in Brazil*. But Arns did much more than publicly oppose regime excesses. He provided legitimacy to the growing movement within civil society against the dictatorship.

New Catholic groups, organized locally in so-called Ecclesiastical Base Communities, which were essentially informal churches located in the growing peripheries of Brazil's largest cities, connected the increasingly progressive politics of leaders like Arns to working-class and poor Brazilians. Those connections between so-called New Labor and the Church created a symbiotic relationship that bolstered two potent regime critics. Arns and other Catholic leaders gave the auto workers their stamp of approval as nonradical, and those workers blessed Church leaders as legitimate opponents of the dictatorship. That mattered because of the history of cooptation and support for authoritarianism by Brazil's religious leaders.

The Church hierarchy had a long history of supporting everyone from the Emperor to Vargas during the Estado Novo, but changes in the Catholic Church over the course of the 1960s led bishops throughout Latin America to embrace what they termed "the option for the poor." The growth of what would become known as Liberation Theology played an important role in solidifying opposition to the Brazilian military dictatorship. The Church joined other established parts of civil society, such as lawyers and journalists, in critiquing the regime. These groups made common cause with an increasingly radicalized student movement and leaders of the New Unionism. Women, who were inspired by second-wave feminism through direct participation in feminist groups abroad while in exile or in Brazil itself, connected with this growing opposition.

Geisel was well aware of this growing opposition and the ways DIEESE and the Church had eroded the regime's legitimacy. He invited the Harvard political scientist Samuel Huntington to Brazil to study how the military could eventually open or "liberalize" society. Huntington visited in 1972 and 1974 to study the situation, and he advised the regime to "decompress" civil society. He made the analogy that Brazilian politics was like a pressure cooker that needed to let off increasing amounts of steam to alleviate pressure on the regime. This was a largely unworkable framework because it failed to address Brazil's future beyond the immediate calming of the political environment. But Huntington's presence at the request of the regime pointed to a significant pivot by Geisel and the ruling generals. They had begun by promising to practice "the politics of anti-politics" in order to preside over a classically liberal capitalist economy. By the late 1960s, the military had abandoned laissez-faire capitalism, and inserted the government into nearly every sector of the economy. And, in the mid-1970s, it began the process of organizing its exit from power.

The military took control of this process, and no longer relied on foreign academics and consultants. In 1979, General João Batista Figueiredo took office as the last military president of his era. The economy continued to suffer from the impact of historically high oil prices, as well as the substantial public debt accumulated by the military since 1964. As much as Médici, and to some extent Geisel, had embraced economic growth as proof of the military's success in running the country, record high rates of inflation and low growth damned the Figueiredo government. The new administration instead focused on the military's now inevitable exit from power. Gone was Huntington's "decompression," and in its place Figueiredo spoke of the *Abertura* or Opening. Like the lens of a mechanical camera with a steadily, slowly increasing aperture, the Brazilian political scene would methodically, under the generals' guidance, transition from military to civilian rule. The original plan assumed the nation would return to the status quo ante, and that the military would face no legal consequences for its many human rights violations, including torture and murder.

The generals assumed there could be no investigations or trials because, in their minds at least, they had always acted legally. The point of the Institutional Acts was to make sure that everything the regime did was technically legal. They also sought to use the controlled process of the *Abertura* to retain the military's institutional integrity. By having public declarations of what the contours of the regime's authority actually were, the military's command structure and hierarchy would not be undermined by the violence it visited upon the population. And the military had some success in this regard. The data on the numbers of people arrested, tortured, and murdered are debated, but the levels are much lower than in other Latin American nations under military dictatorship.

Any incident of torture is a gross violation of human rights, and detaining and questioning people without due process violates civil rights. Murders, especially politically motivated killings, are horrific and inhumane acts. The military has largely avoided having to account for these vicious abuses of power. A series of truth commissions have identified the minimum number of murders and torture victims. Over the course of Brazil's 21-year military dictatorship, about 50,000 people were detained and questioned. The military tortured many of those people. At least 191 have been identified as having been murdered by the regime, and 243 are presumed dead because they were "disappeared" by the military. These totals, however, pale in comparison with the widespread torture and political murder in Argentina and Chile, which had significantly smaller populations than Brazil's 120.7 million people in 1980. Estimates for Argentina's so-called Dirty War are from 15,000 to20,000 people murdered/disappeared out of a total population of 27.9 million in 1980; Augusto Pinochet in Chile oversaw the torture of more than 27,000 people with at least 2,279 documented political murders in a country of about 12.26 million in 1985.

Despite assuring themselves and others that they had acted legally, Brazil's military leaders also turned to their civilian allies in the legislature to pass an amnesty law in 1979 to shield them from later prosecutions. Over the course of the *Abertura*, the military government struggled to maintain control of the process. The generals wanted to engineer their exit, and leave power with civilian politicians in the ARENA party. In fact, Figueiredo's plan for presidential elections called for a legislative vote to choose Brazil's next leader. With ARENA in the majority, the generals were confident that these indirect elections would provide a smooth path to continued conservative rule. The government next decreed changes in the political system to maintain its control. Gubernatorial and state legislative elections had shown increasing support for opposition politicians in the MDB. The Figueiredo administration understood that popular dissatisfaction with the dictatorship was channeled electorally into the catch-all opposition of the MDB, so the regime mandated that all existing parties adopt new names. The government claimed that this was about returning to civilian rule, but it was more an attempt to weaken the opposition MDB by having its various factions splinter into a number of disparate parties. Following this decree, the pro-military ARENA became the Democratic Social Party (Partido Democrático Social or PDS), but the MDB simply added the word *"Partido"* to its name to become the PMDB or Party of the Brazilian Democratic Movement.

New Labor and a New Politics

The PMDB had competing ideological and personalist factions, but it remained unified as the opposition to the regime. The newly named PDS, meanwhile, still retained a slim majority in the legislature, which would indirectly elect Brazil's first civilian president in over two decades. The problem for the regime was that the New Social Movements, along with other actors in civil society, increasingly sought to push the *Abertura* to be more democratic. No group did more to challenge the status quo than industrial workers in the automobile sector. Their organizing activities in the unions, strikes, and direct negotiations with the multinational auto companies pushed Brazil toward an increasingly democratic politics. These workers did so with increasingly effective political ties to the other New Social Movements, particularly the progressive members of the Catholic Church.

Beginning in May 1978, metalworkers in São Paulo's industrial suburbs struck outside the legal, corporatist framework. They backed up their wage demands with data from DIEESE. That fact, the political ties they had made to other social movements, and a long-held national belief that workers in the auto sector were different from previous labor groups helped them garner broad popular support. Establishment newspapers and magazines that had carefully avoided the wrath of government censors openly supported the striking workers. The television networks, which had come of age under the dictatorship and worked closely with it, also editorialized in favor of them. There were even members of the military leadership who spoke positively about the modern, democratic spirit of these workers. Leaders of the foreign auto companies' industrial relations departments reported back to Detroit, Dearborn, Wolfsberg, and Turin that the strikers were no different from North American and European auto workers. The US Secretary of Labor, Ray Marshall, personally told President Jimmy Carter that these strikers had more in common with workers in the United Auto Workers than their populist and communist predecessors in Brazil.

Brazil's auto workers, beginning with this first strike in May 1978 through the early 1980s, led the way for an increasingly assertive civil society that demanded not only that the military leave politics, but also that the nation adopt some form of democracy immediately. The opposition won convincing victories in state elections in 1982, and that brought calls for accelerating the military's exit. This demand became the "*Diretas Já*" or "Direct Elections Now" movement. People across the country took their cues from the successful auto workers' direct action and went to the streets in increasing numbers to demand a popular vote for Brazil's next president. Rallies of more than 1 million people in Rio and 1.5 million in São Paulo made clear the public hunger for electing their next president.

In addition to these popular public demonstrations, actors, athletes, and other well-known figures now openly called for direct elections. One of the most startling developments was the move by Brazil's most-watched television network, Globo (Rede Globo). Its nightly news program, *Jornal Nacional*, increasingly reported favorably on the public mobilizations for direct elections. At the same time, the machinations within the pro-military PDS further soured the populace on the idea of indirect, congressional elections for president. Paulo Maluf, the PDS governor of São Paulo, who was seen as both corrupt and unlikable, managed to become the regime's candidate. His abrasive style, combined with the obvious national desire for change, led one of the regime's most loyal supporters in the Congress, José Sarney, to defect from his leadership role in the PDS to form another party, the Liberal Democratic Front (Partido da Frente Liberal or PFL). Members of the PFL moved away from Maluf and the PDS to back the PMDB's candidate, Tancredo Neves. Neves had entered politics from his home state of Minas Gerais during the Old Republic, and went on to serve in the second Vargas administration's cabinet in the early 1950s. He was a moderate and trustworthy opposition legislator. Between the PMDB's block of votes and those from the newly formed PFL, he was elected on January 15, 1985, to be the first civilian president since the coup. Figueiredo may not have given ground to the *Diretas Já* movement, but the Brazilian people got the indirectly elected president they wanted.

The tumult of the presidential vote was in many ways a fitting end to more than two decades of military rule. The generals had come to power promising to enact technocratic solutions to the problems of the nation's debt and high inflation. They considered themselves to be practitioners of laissez-faire. At the end of 21 years of military rule, the national debt had ballooned in real terms to many times that of 1964, hyper-inflation seemed beyond control, and the state was an active participant in the national economy. The military had also transformed itself from a largely respected national institution to one few in Brazil trusted.

The dictatorship managed to make progress in a number of important areas. It deepened the work begun by Vargas and accelerated by Kubitschek by furthering the physical integration of the nation. It continued to build roads and promote automobility. The regime's controversial Amazonian development program brought about horrific levels of environmental degradation, but it also connected Brazil's far-flung North to the Center-South. The military government also supported the growth of television networks that further connected the nation, and helped to foster a broader sense of Brazilianness. The proliferation of news programs and soap operas (*telenovelas*) was central in this process, but so too was the ability of most

Brazilians to watch their national team in a series of largely successful international soccer tournaments, including the World Cup victory in 1970.

The military dictatorship produced two additional changes to Brazil that few people understood at the time. The first was that the generals had dramatically curtailed the Brazilian penchant for personalistic politics. The regime was a bureaucratic authoritarian government. Although individual generals became president, there was never a cult of personality around those men. Moreover, there were few broadly supported civilian political figures by the early 1980s. The former populist governor of Rio Grande do Sul, who was also João Goulart's brother-in-law, was one exception. Leonel Brizola was broadly popular, but he did not manage to gain the PMDB candidacy for president. The party chose Tancredo Neves as a staid, institutional representative of the broad movement of opposition to the regime. Maluf was far from a popular figure. He, too, represented the politics of the ARENA/PDS more than a broad conservative movement.

The military's other, unexpected contribution to Brazil's national development was its promotion of a deeper and broader sense of democracy among the population. The generals did not set out to create a democratic praxis among the population, but the long dictatorship did just that. Since the 1890s, some Brazilians could vote in some elections. With the exception of the 1930–45 period, there were always some highly circumscribed elections with a tiny portion of the population eligible to vote. The dictatorship changed attitudes about the limited franchise by democratizing repression. Rich and poor alike were denied their civil rights. Conservative politicians, even those closely allied to the regime, had limited political power. Torture and other horrible human rights violations were no longer reserved for the poor. University students and professionals were now also targets of government violence. Those changes, along with more than two decades of dictatorship, clarified for many Brazilians what democracy should look like. Democracy should include the sorts of strikes launched by São Paulo's metalworkers and the popular mobilizations around the *Diretas Já* movement. Most of all, democracy in Brazil would be the opposite of the military dictatorship. That vision, along with the organizational effervescence of the New Social Movements, would shape Brazil's new democracy going forward.

4
Chaotic Democracy (1985–1994)

The euphoria around Tancredo Neves's election belied the complexity and tenuousness of the political situation in Brazil in early 1985. The PMDB gained power through an uneasy alliance with the PFL, which had only just been formed as a breakaway party from the pro-military PDS. In order to secure support from the PFL, Tancredo, as he was known, agreed to make the PFL's José Sarney his vice presidential candidate. But this electoral alliance was even more complicated than that. The PMDB itself was little more than an umbrella party for groups ranging from right of center to the far left. The election of Tancredo Neves and José Sarney had plenty of built-in challenges, and then tragedy struck. Tancredo died before being able to take office. His death, the ascension to power of Sarney as the head of a government filled with politicians he had recently opposed, and the high inflation and low growth that seemed baked into the Brazilian economy led to a chaotic era as Brazil made the transition to what quickly became known as the New Republic. That first decade after the years of military dictatorship redefined Brazilian politics in both positive and negative ways, and it brought literally millions of citizens into the formal electoral system for the first time in the nation's history.

Tancredo Neves hid his illness even from his closest advisors. He did so out of fear that questions about his health could derail the military's exit from power. He was so sick that he finally entered the hospital in São Paulo in March, and he underwent seven separate abdominal surgeries related to a tumor. He died on April 21, 1985, from a post-operative infection. Brazilians, who had had little idea of what was happening, quickly went from feeling jubilant about the end of the dictatorship to having a sense of dread about their nation's future. Sarney had been sworn in as Brazil's vice president on March 15. Tancredo only announced his illness that day to make sure that Sarney could become the vice president and govern as a civilian while he recovered. After Tancredo died, Sarney automatically became Brazil's first civilian president since March 1964.

Democracy's Awkward Beginnings

With the formal transition complete, Sarney and PMDB politicians in the legislature had to begin to govern. They agreed that their first task, which had been laid out by Tancredo, was to write a new constitution. What would become the constitution of 1988 was Brazil's seventh since independence in 1822. It served as both a broad framework for federal governance and a set of specific laws and requirements.

In March 1985, few in Brazil knew what form it would take. Some hoped to establish a parliamentary system, while others embraced the previous structure of a president and a bicameral legislature. There were even a few oddball ideas, including bringing back the descendants of Pedro II to establish a constitutional monarchy. Sarney and the PMDB decided to settle these issues democratically. They began the process of writing a new constitution, which is known in Portuguese as the *Constituente*, by calling for elections for a new legislative body to craft the new document. They held a national election in November 1986 for the Constitutional Assembly, which began its work in February 1987.

Thirteen parties had representatives elected to the 559 member Assembly, but the PMDB dominated with 303 (or 54%) of those seats. The military's former allies in the PFL had the second most members with 135 elected, and the remnants of the pro-military PDS polled third with 38. Two populist parties, Leonel Brizola's Democratic Labor Party (Partido Democrático Trabalhista or PDT) and Vargas's old Labor Party, the PTB, elected 26 and 18 members respectively. The remnants of the old left had only a handful of seats. The Brazilian Communist Party (PCB), which was affiliated with Moscow, elected three people to the Constitutional Assembly, and the Maoist Community Party of Brazil (PC do B) had another three. Beyond the dominance of the PMDB, the appearance of a new political party was also noteworthy. The Workers' Party

(PT) sent 16 people to the Constitutional Assembly. Auto workers in São Paulo's industrial suburbs had founded the party in 1980 with a distinct political orientation that would profoundly affect Brazil's transition to democracy.

In many ways, the PT was more than just a political vehicle for New Labor. Its founders, particularly the charismatic union leader Luiz Inácio Lula da Silva (who is widely known simply as Lula), rejected the politics of the establishment union-oriented parties such as the PTB and PDT, as well as the traditional left of the PCB and PC do B. The PT viewed the former as too tied to the state corporatist labor structure and its system of corrupted union bosses. They rejected the latter for the lack of focus on wage and work issues by the communist parties. Most of all, however, the PT considered itself a party of the new social movements. Its leaders rejected the traditional populist and left parties as hierarchical and undemocratic. The PT would practice internal democratic politics to help foster a broader democratic Brazil. The party initially focused on having only working people and the poor in its ranks. At this point in its history, PT leaders forcefully rejected the idea that intellectuals and professional politicians might influence policy making.

Few in early 1987 grasped how important the PT would become over the next three decades. At the start of the Constitutional Assembly, power rested with the diverse PMDB and Brazil's civilian president from the PFL, who only held office because of the sudden death of the PMDB's leader, Tancredo Neves. The Big Center (*Centrão*) of the parties that had been part of the legislature during the dictatorship (PMDB, PDS, PFL, PTB) dominated the Assembly, and produced a new constitution that simultaneously broke new ground in terms of personal rights, but also remained anchored in the previous era of civilian politics. Like the 1946 constitution, it called for a president and a bicameral legislature, but it also created new personal civil liberties and voting rights. For the first time in Brazil, the constitution guaranteed individual rights and provided for punishment of government actors who infringed upon them. Many of those civil liberties were explicitly articulated as reactions against two decades of dictatorship. The franchise was now universal and voting mandatory. There were no more literacy or other restrictions on who could vote. In fact, everyone 16 years and older was compelled to vote, or they would face a series of fines.

Although PT representatives made up a tiny minority of the Constitutional Assembly, the party's nascent ideology influenced the Assembly in significant ways. Activists from the unions had long argued that civilian government should not be the end goal in and of itself. They said a democracy had to be measured by how it served the people. The 1988 constitution, in addition to making the vote mandatory, provided for referenda, plebiscites, and even citizen-proposed laws. But the constitution was also fairly conservative in several significant ways. The Senate was the most obvious example of minority rule. Brazil's states are binary in terms of population and wealth. About one-third of them have large populations, with the remaining two-thirds being sparsely populated. And the military government created new states in sparsely populated regions in Amazonia. It made Mato Grosso do Sul a state in 1977 and Rondônia one in 1981. The 1988 constitution, written by civilian politicians, then added Amapá, Roraima, and Tocantins. The federal district and each of Brazil's 26 states, no matter their populations, had three senators. Membership in the Chamber of Deputies was set by population, and so was more democratic.

Critics also pointed out that the ways the judiciary was structured, along with the ongoing power of the federal bureaucracy, could limit democratic practice. Still, the Constitutional Assembly produced the most democratic set of laws in the century since the 1889 end of the Empire. It even sought to limit personalistic politics by restricting the presidency to one term at a time (someone could seek reelection after leaving office). This was understood to be a check on an individual's power, and Sarney did not oppose it per se, but he did bargain actively for a five-year term, arguing he needed the extra year in order to set the nation on a new, democratic course. The horse trading over the presidential term between Sarney and PMDB leaders, particularly its leader in the Constitutional Assembly, Ulysses Guimarães, revealed the ugly side of open politics. Guimarães not only drove a hard bargain, he also expressed a good deal of ill will toward Sarney. Many in the PMDB had argued that Guimarães, as the highest-ranking politician in the party, should have become president when Tancredo could not, and Sarney had not yet been sworn in. This argument had little broad appeal, but it underscored the level of animosity between the majority party and the president who took office in the name of that party, although he had never been a member of it.

During the work of the Constitutional Assembly, Brazil operated as a democracy, but under the old constitution. Legislative elections held in 1986 reflected the mood of the nation, with the PMDB dominating in both the upper and lower chambers. In 1986, the PMDB held 48% of the seats in the Chamber of Deputies, and 38 of the 49 total Senate seats, or 78% of the total (this was before the redesign of the Senate according to the 1988 constitution). Over the next four years, however, the coalition that made up the PMDB fractured, and new parties came on the scene. There were three forces at work. The first was a reassertion of personalistic politics that undermined the broad anti-military coalitions. A handful of powerful political figures created new parties that were little more than instruments for their electoral fortunes. They had no real structure beyond that. Then, there were traditional political parties that sought to regain prominent places in the system. They were parties, but with a personalistic tilt given their history. Finally, new actors in politics sought to institutionalize the social movements from the dictatorship. The most effective and powerful centered on the new unionism movement, which led to the creation of the PT in 1980. But even this new party, which developed a complex institutional framework, was often popularly associated with its charismatic leader, Lula.

These dynamics played out while Sarney and the legislature sought to govern democratic Brazil, while at the same time the Constitutional Assembly wrote a new guiding document for the country's politics going forward. Sarney spent most of his political capital on two very different projects. For himself, he lobbied tirelessly for a five-year presidential term. For Brazil, he attempted to contain inflation, which had reached 226% in 1985, with a package of price freezes, wage increases, and a new currency. The Cruzado Plan, which Sarney proposed and was approved overwhelmingly by the legislature, froze prices for fuels, rents, and most consumer goods on February 28, 1986. Soon after setting these prices and creating government price indices, Brasília released a new currency, the cruzado. A single cruzado held the same value as 1,000 cruzeiros. At first, the government simply stamped the new value on older currency, which highlighted the great disparity. Soon new cruzado bills were introduced into the economy. The government next mandated wage increases of around 8% tied to the new currency. It increased the minimum wage by 18%. With prices frozen and wages increased, Brazilians went on spending sprees, and the government basked in popular support for this intervention in the economy. Although inflation for the year was 146%, the monthly rate dropped from 12.5% at the start of the plan in February 1986 to 1.4% in October. Fixed prices and increased wages brought about a completely new problem: shortages of goods, often driven by producers' unwillingness to sell their products at prices they did not like.

The initial euphoria over the Cruzado Plan gave way to frustration as groceries and other goods grew increasingly scarce throughout the nation. At the same time, Brazilians seemed to move beyond the excitement and sense of hope around the end of the dictatorship. They wanted their democracy to deliver tangible results. The 1990 elections revealed the changing national mood during this move from the transition out of dictatorship to a democratic society. While the PMDB remained the largest party in both houses, it did so in a significantly diminished way. Thirty-three parties ran candidates for the Chamber of Deputies, and 14 of them succeeded in electing members. PMDB candidates received the highest vote totals, and got about 19% of the seats, followed by the PFL with about 12%, and the PT with 10%. The Senate saw the PMDB and PFL each with eight seats, and senators from nine other parties and one independent made up the rest. The proliferation of new parties did not signal a move toward a more institutionalized politics, however. Often, they were cobbled together by a few individuals as personal electoral vehicles. They did not invest in party building, and there were few structures beyond offices in Brasília and a handful of state capitals.

The Workers' Party was a complicated exception to this development. Its origins in the New Social Movements shaped the party from its founding in 1980 onward. The PT emphasized internal democracy, and so created a series of local and state-level parties in order to represent its rank-and-file. The Workers' Party operated in reaction against the traditional ways in which politics had functioned in Brazil. Just as the metalworkers in São Paulo's industrial suburbs had rejected the hierarchical, corporatist labor structure that privileged a few leaders over the majority of working people, the PT sought to build a broad, popular political party. And, perhaps more than any party in Brazil's history, it did build up structures that led to the election of mayors, state legislators, and governors in states nationwide. Despite this impressive institutionalization of popular power, however, the PT was often identified more with Lula's charisma than anything else. The tension between Lula's personal appeal and the PT's broad base would be both a blessing and a curse over the course of the following three decades.

The Return of Personalistic Politics

With the new constitution in place, and the Cruzado Plan's wage and price controls ended, Brazilians began to think about the nation's first open, direct election for president, which would take place in 1989. The PT's growth and success led many observers to begin to think that Lula could be Brazil's next leader. While the outcome could not be predicted, what was obvious was that the campaign would be a free for all of candidates and parties. In an effort to make the process more open, there was a set time of the day for political advertisements on television in order to lessen the influence of money in the system. Parties that reached a minimum status in public polling received free airtime during the electoral hour each night. It is hard to gauge the effectiveness of this system, and there were many press reports of increases in video rentals and other activities during the so-called election hour each evening. Still, the use of such a device demonstrated how Brazilians in the post-dictatorship period tried to think through the ways in which they could make their system as democratic as possible.

The election was scheduled for November 15, 1989, which was the one hundredth anniversary of the fall of the Empire and the technical start of republican politics in Brazil. If no one achieved a majority of the votes, which would be difficult if not impossible with 22 candidates on the ballot, a second round of voting between the top two would take place the following month on December 17. Some of the candidates were familiar, as were some of the parties. Beyond the PT's Lula, Paulo Maluf was back running as the leader of the PDS. The popular former governor of Rio Grande do Sul (1959–63) and later of Rio de Janeiro (1983–87), Leonel Brizola, ran as the head of the party he had founded, the Democratic Labor Party or PDT. Ulysses Guimarães, who served as the powerful president of the Chamber of Deputies, ran as the PMDB standard bearer. Lesser-known politicians ran as the heads of well-established parties such as the PTB, PCB, and PFL. A host of new parties also put forward candidates, but three men dominated the polling on November 15: Lula won 17.19% of the vote, Brizola had 16.51%, and a new figure on the national scene, Fernando Collor de Mello, received 30.48%. Brizola represented the populist past to many Brazilians given his ties to João Goulart, and perhaps because of that, he failed to reach the second round. The top two vote getters, Lula and Collor de Mello, appeared to symbolize a new fault line in Brazilian politics.

Collor de Mello sold himself as a new man for what was increasingly known as Brazil's New Republic. He ran as the leader of the recently created National Reconstruction Party (Partido de Reconstrução Nacional or PRN), which came into existence in 1985 as the Youth Party (Partido de Juventude or PJ) and changed its name in time for the presidential election. Collor de Mello ran for president while serving as the governor of the tiny Northeastern state of Alagoas. He had few accomplishments in his brief gubernatorial tenure (he took the oath of office in March 1987), but he was in fact the scion of a powerful political family with roots in the Old Republic. His father was a senator, and his grandfather was Lindolfo Collor, Vargas's first Minister of Labor. Although only four years younger than Lula, the 40-year-old Collor de Mello often jogged in public to emphasize his vigor.

Collor de Mello ran as a youthful outsider, but he actually represented the interests of many of the most powerful institutions in Brazil. As such, he became the standard bearer for the growing push for neoliberal solutions for stagnating Latin American economies. The drive to privatize state-run industries and utilities and to liberalize trade had begun in Chile under the military dictatorship of Augusto Pinochet (1973–90), and then gained momentum after the 1984 peso crisis in Mexico. In response to Mexico's inability to pay even the interest on its massive foreign debt, Ronald Reagan's administration (1981–9) pushed the country and others in Latin America to liberalize trade and open their economies. During the administration of George H.W. Bush (1989–93), Secretary of the Treasury Nicholas Brady created a series of specialized bonds to assist Latin American nations with their foreign debt. Acceptance of these so-called Brady bonds required Mexico to open its economy to more foreign investment, and to move toward freer trade. This process culminated with the signing of the North American Free Trade Agreement (NAFTA) among Mexico, the United States, and Canada, which went into effect on January 1, 1994.

Collor de Mello's campaign, although aggressively backed by corporate interests that had flourished under the military's tutelage, echoed these policies and so called for the removal of many barriers to free trade, the removal of the national government from much of the economy with an associated privatization of state-run industries, and a major reorganization of the federal bureaucracy. These plans reflected the neoliberal zeitgeist of the time in Latin America, and they were promoted as being a counterweight to leftist politics, even though in many cases in the region – and especially in Brazil – they sought to dismantle the economic policies put in place by a conservative military dictatorship. That idea was heavily promoted by the media, especially by the most powerful Brazilian news outlet, the Globo Network, through its popular nightly news program, *Jornal Nacional*.

The electoral hour had been created to level the playing field by allotting set times for political advertising on television. But once major news outlets tacitly endorsed Collor de Mello's candidacy, the balance and access implied by the electoral hour became more fiction than reality. Globo spearheaded the coverage of Collor de Mello as a youthful outsider bringing fresh ideas to the nation. The network, in turn, painted Lula as a combination of a populist and communist who was somehow responsible for the nation's hyperinflation, estimated at 90% per month, while it glossed over Collor de Mello's ties to the very businesses – such as Globo itself – that had flourished by working closely with statist military policy makers. This preference for Collor de Mello broke into the open just days before voting in the runoff. Abilio Diniz, one of Brazil's wealthiest people, was kidnapped in early December. He was held by a group of radical revolutionaries, including two Canadian citizens, who sought to use ransom money to help fund the Sandinistas in Nicaragua. Globo and other news outlets breathlessly covered the kidnapping and Diniz's eventual police rescue. The media painted the kidnapping as the sort of thing Brazilians could expect under Lula and the PT. Brazil's strict electoral law banned the party and candidates from commenting days before the voting, and so the media's anti-Lula spin succeeded in poisoning the well for the PT.

Lula's entire career in union and electoral politics had focused on promoting democracy and eschewing the sort of violent, revolutionary activities of Diniz's kidnappers. His 1989 platform was a Brazilian version of classic social democratic politics. In contrast to Collor de Mello, the PT did not call for the dismantling of the state and aggressive privatizations. Instead, Lula's campaign posed a question based in the PT's founding from the New Social Movements: how could a real democracy produce the outcomes that Brazil was experiencing? How could one explain support for policies that left more than half of its citizens living in poverty? In other words, for Brazil's democracy to function properly, policy outcomes should match popular expectations. The PT crystalized this idea in its campaign slogan, "Without Fear of Being Happy." What made the PT so different from previous liberal and left parties was that it was willing to experiment with public policy. Neither Lula nor the party was against private enterprise per se; most of the party leadership had worked for multinational automobile manufacturers, where they received some of the highest salaries and best benefits paid to Brazilian workers. The PT simply sought to bring the social democratic politics of several Western European nations to Brazil.

The PT's belief in internal democracy meant that the opinions of the rank-and-file shaped its electoral platforms. Activists in the party often embraced policies that were more radical than many in Brazil would accept. During the writing of the new constitution, the PT demanded a rejection of Brazil's foreign debt. Many in the party called for the nationalization of banks and natural resources, and the PT formally advocated for a broad agrarian reform. These political positions, along with the relentlessly critical coverage by Globo and other corporate media, put the PT on the defensive as the second round of presidential voting loomed. The Diniz kidnaping was the near perfect final act in painting the PT as too radical for Brazil. And so, despite Lula's personal popularity and the creation of a coherent national party structure, Collor de Mello prevailed in the polling on December 17, with 53% of the vote to Lula's 47%.

When Collor de Mello took the oath of office on March 15, 1990, Brazil was again in the midst of seemingly uncontrollable inflation. Estimates of the rates fluctuated wildly from 25% to 90% per month.

Despite this economic uncertainty, Brazilians had high expectations for their New Republic. Collor de Mello and his vice president, the Mineiro politician Itamar Franco, were the first popularly elected Brazilian leaders to take office since Jânio Quadros and João Goulart were sworn in on January 31, 1961. With expectations high, the new administration got to work quickly by issuing a currency stabilization plan (the Collor Plan), planning a series of privatizations of utilities (especially in the telecommunications sector), and initiating a thorough reorganization of the federal bureaucracy. The new president had some early successes, but was limited by the complexity of Brazil's challenges in the early years of the New Republic.

Collor de Mello tried to demonstrate both administrative competence and a sense that his government could exert real control over the nation with his attempt to bring down hyperinflation. Although the administration worked to decrease the government's role in the economy, the Collor Plan literally froze 80% of privately held bank holdings, and forcibly converted them into bonds bearing 6% interest. This was to last 18 months in order to reduce the money supply and stem inflation. The economic carrot to this stick was a broad, if initially slow, program of trade liberalization with a floating exchange rate. The administration also shrunk the federal bureaucracy by roughly 300,000 jobs. The Collor Plan had mixed results. Inflation initially came down, but then began to rise after a few months. Its greatest success was in shifting policy toward neoliberal solutions. In addition to opening markets to more foreign competition, the Collor de Mello administration began the process of privatization of state-run industries, none more prominent than the national steel company at Volta Redonda. This began a process that would continue throughout the 1990s, and include the auctioning off of the various state telephone companies, along with the spectrum for cellular telephony.

Collor de Mello did not have a broad mandate for these privatizations, and his monetary policies enraged many businesses whose accounts had been frozen and temporarily transferred into non-fungible bonds. He therefore avoided the legislature, and instead operated through a series of presidential decrees that could only stand for 30 days if they were not ratified by a congressional vote. When his policies failed to receive that support, Collor de Mello simply reissued the decrees. He did this because he had to contend with a legislature made of up of members of 19 separate parties in the Chamber of Deputies, and 12 in the Senate. And even within parties, there was often little policy cohesion or discipline. The PT was regularly an exception, but it only held 35 seats in the Chamber and one in the Senate. Overall, both legislative houses were collections of individuals who were more often than not interested in securing patronage and other funding for themselves, their families, and their districts and/or states. Next to Collor de Mello, the President of the Chamber of Deputies was the most powerful political figure in the nation. The Paulista politician Ulysses Guimarães had steered the legislature so well in the immediate aftermath of the dictatorship on behalf of the PMDB majority that he ran for president in 1989. Having failed to make the run-off, he left the scene and a series of much less talented men tried to bring order to Brazil's lower house. Without a strong hand at the helm, and with a presidential administration moving to privatize a steadily increasing number of state-owned firms, patronage and graft dominated the legislative session. The many problems posed by this disorganization and corruption could have strengthened the president's hand had he himself not outdone the nation's legislators through previously unheard of levels of profiteering and dishonesty.

Scandal, Impeachment, and the Constitutional Order

Corruption is not unique to any one country or type of political system. It exists everywhere, but it is often worse where governments play a large role in the economy, and it is especially bad where there is a weak judiciary. Brazil at the start of the New Republic had both an economy closely tied to the state and a weak system of investigations, prosecutions, and overall judicial oversight. That environment and a legislature filled with politicians without strong party or institutional ties led to a great deal of legal and illegal influence peddling, and growing incidents of outright graft. But no matter how broad these problems were in the legislature, it was the newly elected president and his family who undertook a brazen corruption scheme larger than anything previously discovered in Brazilian history. The obscene levels of theft were truly a family affair.

Brasília-based journalists quickly noticed unusually high levels of spending by the president's family, including his wife's frequent purchases of haute couture and a massive landscaping project at their personal residence. What those reporters discovered was that soon after the election, Collor de Mello's campaign's treasurer, Paulo César Farias, who was known simply as PC, had set up a series of dummy corporations to funnel bribes from corporate interests and others for political favors. Estimates vary on the total amount of money involved, with a low of about $9 million, while some journalists believe the total to be several times that. The president tried to ignore the growing scandal, hoping that people would simply see it as business as usual in the nation's capital. In May 1992, when the president's brother, Pedro Collor, accused the president of benefiting from a massive influence peddling scheme orchestrated by his campaign manager, the crisis engulfed both the presidency and the very fabric of the New Republic.

Pedro Collor publicly accused PC of bringing in millions of dollars in graft, which he then divided 70–30 between the president and himself. This massive corruption further enraged a public who had had their bank accounts frozen and continued to suffer through spiraling rates of inflation. Legislators who did not want a newly energized press looking more broadly at corruption, and who had little sense of allegiance to Collor de Mello, joined the chorus of denunciations of the president and his family. With a steady stream of breaking news about presidential malfeasance, popular pressure built for Collor de Mello's impeachment. In July, federal authorities opened a formal investigation and the Congress created a Joint Parliamentary Commission of Inquiry on the matter. A month later, the president went on national television to denounce the attempts to remove him. He asked that Brazilians wear the national colors of green, yellow, and blue to show their support for him. The media reported in the days after his speech that people throughout the nation instead wore black, and held signs demanding Collor de Mello leave office.

Formal impeachment proceedings began over several weeks in September. On September 29, the Chamber of Deputies easily cleared the two-thirds requirement to impeach Collor de Mello with a vote of 441 deputies in favor and only 38 opposed. The Senate then took up the matter, and formally declared the president to be a defendant in an impeachment trial, which triggered a constitutional requirement that he lose his executive authority for 180 days. Itamar Franco, the vice president, took on the responsibilities of the chief executive. With significant evidence of wrongdoing and popular and political sentiment against him, Collor de Mello resigned the presidency on December 29, 1992, which was the final day of the Senate proceedings. Although he had left office, he was not finished with either the Senate trial or ongoing judicial proceedings. Many throughout the nation felt as though the impeachment should be completed to fulfill the constitutional procedure, and so the Senate voted 76 to three to convict him (two senators did not participate). That vote triggered a constitutional requirement that Collor de Mello be stripped of his political rights for eight years.

At first glance, the system had worked well: a free and aggressive press had initially uncovered the president's massive graft and both houses of the legislature followed the constitutional procedures in moving to impeach him. Even after he stepped down, the Senate continued its work to make sure the process worked as planned. Brazilian voters paid close attention to the scandal, and largely supported the president's impeachment and removal. But even as everything seemed to work as it should, there was a national sense of foreboding about the entire episode. The graft had begun during the election and was run by Collor de Mello's campaign director. Brazilians began to look back at that process and found many flaws in the ways they had elected their president, including the fact that so much of the corporate media had colluded to portray Collor de Mello as a fresh-faced outsider and Lula as a dangerous radical. That re-examination of the 1989 election was consciously and subconsciously contextualized by Brazil's last democratic presidential election three decades earlier. Corruption did not drive Jânio Quadros from office, but his disastrous short presidency, combined with conservative fears of what his vice president, João Goulart, would do once elevated to chief executive, set the stage for a 21-year military dictatorship. The New Republic had begun with its first leader, Tancredo Neves, dying before he could take office. Its first democratically elected leader then left in disgrace. Throughout all of this turmoil, the Brazilian economy was suffering through low growth and high inflation. The chaos of the early 1990s seemed to mirror that of the early 1960s.

Luckily for Brazil, Itamar Franco was nothing like João Goulart in either temperament or ideology. He may have been the ideal individual for the presidency at this moment in time. A civil engineer by training, he entered local politics in his home town of Juiz da Fora in Minas Gerais. He eventually became the mayor, and from there was elected to the Senate in Brasília in 1974, where he became a leader in the opposition MDB and then PMDB. In the years before being elected vice president, and in that office, Franco held liberal but not radical positions on a number of key issues. He sought to break diplomatic relations with South Africa's apartheid regime, and openly acknowledged the deep racism in Brazilian society. He called for the nationalization of subsoil or mining rights, union independence from the Ministry of Labor, better national employment standards, and the decriminalization of abortion, among other things. He had even openly opposed some of Collor de Mello's planned privatizations while vice president. Most significant of all for this juncture, he had always been a fierce critic of corrupt politicians, going so far as to call for the resignation of José Sarney at one point, and maintaining his anti-corruption stance throughout Collor de Mello's administration. Unlike the moment when Quadros resigned and so many political conservatives and even moderates, along with the military's leadership, feared the transition to a Goulart administration, Franco's avuncular presence and moderately liberal politics brought calm and even a sense of relief to the nation.

That sense of near tranquility with the ascension of Franco to the presidency was in direct contrast with the panic many felt about Brazil's ongoing economic woes. Inflation remained not just high, but out of control. The rate of price increases was reported as a monthly not yearly number. Moreover, economic growth remained sluggish at best. GDP was as weak in the first years of the New Republic as it had been during the last years of the dictatorship. During Collor de Mello's administration, it shrunk in 1990, grew by 1% in 1991, and then contracted again in 1992. The World Bank reported that Brazil's annual inflation was astronomical during these years, with rates of 1,430% in 1989 and 2,948% in 1990. Inflation dropped to the still very high 433% in 1991, and then rose to 952% in 1992.

The combination of low and even negative growth with dizzying rates of inflation, along with the political turmoil of Collor de Mello's impeachment, undermined Brazilians' faith in their New Republic. The sense of frustration so many felt in the late 1980s and early 1990s was not unique to this era, however. For most of its modern history, Brazil seemed to be ungovernable. We have already seen how popular turmoil in Rio and regional uprisings forced the country's most powerful landowners to create the fiction of Pedro II's majority in 1840. Then, when the military removed Pedro II and ended the Empire in 1889, millenarian uprisings, unequal development, poor and nonexistent transportation links, and military uprisings revealed just how slow the progress and incomplete the order were during Brazil's Old Republic.

Getúlio Vargas, Juscelino Kubitschek, and the military governments of the dictatorship all sought to bring order and progress to Brazil by increasing the power of the central government. Vargas created a series of new institutions, JK built a new, more centrally located national capital, and the military used both force and bureaucratic expansion to try to gain control of the economy and politics. These moments of central state intervention from the 1840 ascension of Pedro II through the military coup in 1964 brought a temporary sense of relief as national leaders seemed to have gained control over the chaos then gripping

Brazil. Many people hoped that the democratic governance begun in 1985 would somehow solve these long-standing problems, but the disastrous Collor de Mello years made that seem impossible. While Itamar Franco was a popular leader, few had faith that he could bring order, let alone progress, to Brazil. He surprised both his supporters and detractors, however, by turning to an ambitious Paulista politician, Fernando Henrique Cardoso, who shocked many by bringing down inflation and restoring faith in the national economy. By doing so, Cardoso paved the way for close to two decades of economic growth, political stability, and increasing prestige for Brazil on the world stage.

5
The Triumph of Social Democracy (1994–2010)

In the early to mid-1990s, Brazil began a two-decade period of robust economic growth, reasonable levels of inflation, growing administrative competence and bureaucratic expansion, and an increasingly significant role and reputation on the world stage. Two very different men led Brazil through this golden era of political economy. As different as they were in biography, Fernando Henrique Cardoso and Luiz Inácio Lula da Silva were both products of Brazil's political left. Cardoso migrated to the center or even center-right of politics, but the two men's origins and political trajectories illustrate important aspects of Brazilian politics during the dictatorship and early years of the New Republic. Lula became a key figure in national politics through his leadership of the metalworkers' union in the late 1970s and early 1980s. He was the most widely recognized labor leader in Brazilian history, and was the runner-up in the 1989 presidential election. Fernando Henrique Cardoso (or FHC, as he is widely known) had a much more complicated path to political prominence. The lives and political careers of both men shaped Brazil as it seemed to finally stabilize economically and politically under the New Republic.

The Rise of FHC

Fernando Henrique Cardoso was the scion of an affluent Brazilian family with roots in the politics of the Old Republic. He earned his undergraduate and graduate degrees in Sociology from the University of São Paulo (USP). His early work, which was heavily influenced by his doctoral advisor, Florestan Fernandes – a leading Marxist scholar of race and slavery in Brazil – gained him international acclaim. He taught in France, Chile, and at some of the leading research universities in the United States, including Stanford and Berkeley, during the dictatorship. FHC's best-known and most important work is *Dependency and Development in Latin America* (1969), which he co-authored with the Chilean scholar Enzo Faletto. The book has been broadly translated, and it is considered one of the most influential works in dependency theory, which argues that the unequal trade relations between Western Europe and the United States, on the one hand, and the Global South, on the other, actively undermined the economic development of Latin America, Africa, and much of Asia. Although written from a Marxist perspective, it helped to justify direct government support for domestic industry with subsidies, high tariffs, and other trade policies.

Cardoso returned to Brazil during the *Abertura*, and turned to electoral politics. He won a Senate seat from São Paulo in 1982 as a PMDB candidate, and then ran a disastrous mayoral campaign in São Paulo in 1985, losing to former president Jânio Quadros. Elected again to the Senate in 1986, FHC joined the newly created Brazilian Social Democratic Party (Partido da Social Democracia Brasileira or PSDB), which drew its members from the more conservative ranks of the PMDB and from the PSD, which had been the pro-military party during the dictatorship. Cardoso led this new party in the Senate until Itamar Franco asked him to join his cabinet as Brazil's Minister of Foreign Affairs. After less than a year in that post, FHC changed portfolios and became the Minister of Finance in May 1993, where he was tasked with trying to bring order to Brazil's economic mess.

Although he had left academia, Cardoso maintained close ties to the university world through his former colleagues and his wife, Ruth Leite Cardoso, a leading anthropologist at USP. Those connections paid significant dividends when FHC as Minister of Finance turned to the Economics faculty at USP to craft a reform package. The result was yet another new currency and program. The Real Plan of 1994 was named for the new currency (the plural is reais), which was pegged 1:1 to the US dollar. In other words, the new currency had a nominal value of US$1.00, rather than a value set by currency markets. It did not float. The Real Plan attacked what its creators saw as the underlying driver of hyperinflation: so-called inertial inflation. Inertial inflation refers to a situation in which prices for nearly all goods and services rise because they are contractually tied to a price index.

Even inexact predictions of future price increases, which in turn lead to changes in price indices, will drive up actual prices as firms adjust them according to those indices. Ending inertial inflation requires breaking the cycle of increases tied to expectations of future price increases. Pricing goods essentially in dollars through reais was a first step in that process.

The Real Plan also had aggressive fiscal and monetary policies. Government spending decreased and interest rates were increased beginning in March 1994. This brought inflation under control, and also attracted significant new foreign investment. The engineered drop in the rate of inflation seemed to many Brazilians to be miraculous. The government introduced the real in mid-1994. Inflation that year was over 2,000%. It fell all the way down to 66% in 1995, and then reached very reasonable levels going forward. It was 16% in 1996 and 7% in 1997, followed by 3% and 5% in the next two years. In 1994, GDP grew at 5.3%, and then dropped a bit the following year to 4.4%. In 1996, it then was cut in half to 2.2%. While growth was moderate at this time, trade liberalization and foreign investment picked up where domestic production had faltered. The Brazilian public focused on the real's success in taming inflation. The Ministry of Finance made sure people understood that prices were stabilizing by reintroducing coins to the money supply. With hyperinflation seemingly baked into the system, most coin-operated public phones, vending machines, and so forth, used tokens whose prices rose along with the general rate of inflation. Coins could and did replace some of these tokens, and the broad public noticed.

Cardoso's success in gaining control over the economy shaped the 1994 presidential election, even though the real's impact was only just beginning to be felt. The broad public associated the improving economy with FHC, the Minister of Finance, and not the sitting president who had appointed him. Given the nature of Brazilian politics with its weak party structures and tendency toward personalism over policy, 1994 saw another crowded field for the first round of voting in November. The political environment seemed particularly tumultuous because it was a general election with legislative and presidential voting. Fully 18 parties elected candidates to the legislature, and eight men ran in the first round of presidential voting.

Most people expected the presidential balloting to lead to another run-off. FHC ran as the head of the PSDB. Lula again ran as the Workers' Party (PT) candidate. His campaign was undermined by the PT's categorial rejection of the efficacy of the Real Plan, the success of which compromised his candidacy. The governor of São Paulo, Orestes Quércia, ran under the banner of the PMDB, and Leonel Brizola, the populist heir to Jânio Quadros and Getúlio Vargas, again headed the PDT ticket. Quércia and Brizola represented the past to many voters who were eager to look to the future. A relatively unknown physician and mathematician, Enéas Carneiro, ran under the banner of a new party, PRONA (Partido de Reedificação da Ordem Nacional or Party of the Reconstruction of the Nation), which was little more than a vehicle for his personal political ambitions. Carneiro's appeal was that he was new to the political scene. Most observers believed the initial vote would result in a run-off between FHC and Lula. But the strength of the Real Plan and Cardoso's close association with the improving economy, along with the PT's criticism of it, propelled FHC to an unexpected first round victory with 54.28% of the vote. Lula was the only other candidate whose percentage of the vote reached double digits. He won 27% of the total.

One of the clear messages of the 1994 election was that Brazil remained in the grip of personalistic politics. Most voters did not think through the PSDB platform. They simply approved of the job Cardoso had done in taming inflation. Carneiro came in a distant third with 7.4% of the vote. He had a loosely defined set of ideas, and simply ran as an intelligent and highly educated outsider. Quércia, the governor of São Paulo, and the head of the once mighty PMDB, received less than 5% of the national vote. The populist Brizola polled at 3%. Lula did much better than everyone but FHC in part because the PT actually had a party structure, and he was personally quite popular.

Cardoso had been elected as the man who had finally tamed inflation, and the weak party structure and absence of strong political institutions gave him a lot of room to maneuver once he took office on January 1, 1995. He chose to embrace the growing interest in liberalized trade in the Western Hemisphere, and Brazil under his presidency became a key participant in what was increasingly known as "the Washington Consensus." This was a set of 10 neoliberal policy prescriptions for developing economies. First, they should practice fiscal discipline to avoid deficits and debts. That had also been a cornerstone of the Real Plan. Second, the state should redirect public spending from subsidies for domestic industries to support for the poor through programs that would also promote future economic growth, such as primary education, healthcare, and infrastructure. Third, it called for reform to broaden the tax base. Fourth, it required realistic interest rates determined by markets rather than central banks. Related to that, the fifth component of the Washington Consensus was that governments should maintain competitive exchange rates. Sixth, liberalizing trade was a centerpiece of this program, along with providing less protection for domestic industries. Related to that, the seventh component was the liberalization of inward capital flows by removing barriers to most forms of foreign investment. Eighth, countries should privatize state enterprises. The ninth part of the program was an embrace of targeted deregulation. Governments should keep regulations related to safety, environmental, and consumer protections, and there needed to be regulations of financial institutions to encourage foreign investment. And, finally, the tenth issue was a broad guarantee for the legal security of property rights. This was a reaction to previous eras of nationalizations, particularly of natural resources.

The Washington Consensus was completely consistent with FHC's politics, and he had an eager ally in the US president, Bill Clinton, who had recently signed NAFTA with Canada and Mexico. But these policies were not always broadly popular, and Cardoso, like his predecessors, faced a highly balkanized legislature made up of representatives of 18 parties. His administration was technically part of a coalition with other parties, including at one point the PMDB, which still held the most legislative seats, but politicians continued to act more as free agents than a voting bloc. That forced FHC to follow his predecessors and use executive decrees to enact policy. Cardoso did have one major legislative victory with a constitutional amendment. After aggressively trading favors and providing patronage, he made it possible to serve two consecutive terms. One minor compromise was that each term would now be four instead of five years. (There is still no limit on the total number of terms someone can serve as president, but they cannot serve more than two consecutively.)

The Cardoso years are best known for the major changes they brought to the Brazilian economy by embracing much of the Washington Consensus. Although Collor de Mello had been a major proponent of privatizations, his impeachment brought Itamar Franco to office, and he was a much more traditional developmentalist who looked to Cardoso's earlier academic work to support state-owned utilities and other businesses. FHC embraced the neoliberal zeitgeist of the 1990s and pushed to sell off state firms involved in mining and telecommunications. The Companhia Vale do Rio Doce, one of the largest mining companies in the world, was sold off and became simply Vale S.A., with its shares trading on major world exchanges. The national telephone company Telebrás, along with the state affiliates and the growing cellular bandwidth was broken up and sold through a process of sealed bids. The Brazilian government was careful to avoid the obvious corruption that characterized a similar series of privatizations in Mexico.

Privatizations, a stable currency, and a market-driven exchange rate not only attracted foreign investment, they also bolstered domestic capital markets. But Cardoso did not ignore Brazil's impoverished citizens. The dramatic decline in inflation directly improved conditions for the nation's working class and poor. His administration also eventually initiated several programs to address poverty directly. The School, Food, and Cooking Gas grants were direct payment programs to many of the poorest Brazilians. Lula's PT government would dramatically expand these modest programs in the early 2000s. Their significance lay in the fact that Cardoso's government did not embrace a pure neoliberal ideology in policy making that valued only market-based solutions. He and his political allies took seriously the components of the Washington Consensus that called for some government regulation and social/economic interventions.

FHC's administration also sought to address a series of lingering political issues. The president opened formal investigations into many of the worst human rights abuses during the dictatorship, and moved to have the military provide information about its unaccounted-for victims, the "disappeared." He then moved to have those individuals declared legally dead. That not only provided spiritual and emotional closure for many families, it also allowed some to receive life insurance payments they had been denied without legal evidence of a death. It permitted observant Catholic widows and widowers to remarry in the Church. Along with that reckoning, Cardoso issued an additional set of blanket pardons to military officials to attempt to close out that ugly era of Brazil's history. He also used his experiences as a polyglot, internationally known academic and former Foreign Minister to expand Brazil's presence on the world stage. He had particularly close relations with Bill Clinton and Ernesto Zedillo, who served as Mexico's president from 1994 to 2000. Cardoso next built ties to Zedillo's successor, Vicente Fox. They worked as the leaders of Latin America's two most populous nations to temper the post-9/11 policies of the George W. Bush administration in the region.

FHC's popularity propelled him to a relatively easy reelection in 1998. He once again prevailed in the first round of balloting with 53% of the vote as the PSDB candidate, again with Marco Maciel from the PFL as his vice president. Lula came in second for the third time, now with 32%, leading the PT. The next closest candidate was Ciro Gomes, who took 11% of the vote under the banner of the Popular Socialist Party (Partido Popular Socialista or PPS), which contained elements of the defunct Communist Party and other left groups. Once again, the election results did not reflect organizing by political parties and social movements. Brazilian politics remained personalistic, and Cardoso would have won under any party's banner in 1998. The legislature remained highly balkanized, and so the tradition of individual members trading favors and patronage for votes continued. No one in the Brazilian political system had an interest in challenging the status quo; they just continued to work through it no matter how much corruption it produced.

Most of President Cardoso's policies contradicted the politics and worldview of Professor Cardoso from the 1960s and 1970s. There was, however, one set of ideas he never abandoned, and they concerned Brazil's ongoing legacy of racial discrimination based in its history as the world's largest slaveholding society. Near the end of his second term as president in 2001, FHC ordered all federal ministries to develop specific quotas for hiring Afro-Brazilians. He also included a quota system for hiring women in this first iteration of affirmative action in Brazil. A year later, Cardoso decreed a National Affirmative Action Program to extend hiring quotas to companies that did business with the federal government. He also initiated a series of targeted programs to provide special assistance to Afro-Brazilian candidates for highly competitive jobs in the federal government, such as in the Foreign Ministry. These policies used national government programs to begin a process of finally addressing Brazilian racial discrimination. This was also the first time Brazil's leader even spoke to Afro-Brazilians as a group since Vargas had embraced the Frente Negra in the 1930s.

Cardoso, though, was most closely associated with his economic program. The Real Plan had stabilized the Brazilian economy, and the privatizations and trade liberalization fueled growth during much of his presidency. The nation's industrial and agricultural sectors continued to expand, and both contributed to growing export revenues during the 1990s. But Brazil's increasingly liberalized trade also made the nation more susceptible to global economic trends. When the world economy experienced a series of problems, from the Asian financial crisis of mid-1997 to the bursting of the so-called internet bubble a few years later, its economy suffered. While GDP growth reached 3.4% in 1997, it fell to 0.33% and 0.47% in 1998 and 1999. This downturn, along with increasing reports in the media about the government's use of patronage and outright corruption to buy votes in the legislature, led to a significant decline in FHC's personal popularity. The changing popular perceptions of Cardoso and his government, along with the PT's steadfast refusal to join with the center-right and center-left establishment parties, which were increasingly tarred by corruption allegations, opened the door to the possibility that Lula might win the presidency in 2002, which would be his fourth attempt at the office.

An Auto Worker as President

Lula's biography was always an important part of his campaigns for office. His life story resonated with many Brazilians, especially the impoverished and working class. Luiz Inácio da Silva was born in 1945 in a small town in the interior of Pernambuco in Brazil's poverty-stricken Northeast. He was the seventh of eight children in a working-class family. Soon after Lula's birth, his father left for work in the port city of Santos in São Paulo. Seven years later, Lula's mother brought the rest of the family to São Paulo. They traveled on a sort of flatbed truck with a center bar for people to hold onto. Migrating from the economically challenged Northeast to the growing cities in Brazil's Center-South on a so-called Parrot's Perch truck (or *pau de arara*) was common in the 1950s and early 1960s as the nation's roads improved and the automobile industry flourished in and around São Paulo.

As child in the city's industrial suburbs, the young Lula dreamed of working in the factories, given how good the wages and benefits there. He began working without graduating from high school, and eventually did quality control on the factory shop floor.

By the mid-1970s, Lula used the freedom to walk throughout the factory to learn about workers' concerns. He used his familiarity with so many of his fellow auto workers to make his way into the leadership ranks of the metalworkers' union in São Bernardo, which is right outside of the city of São Paulo. His intelligence, experiences, and charisma propelled him into the union's leadership. With the massive strike waves among metalworkers around São Paulo beginning in 1978, Lula increasingly became a national figure who represented what people began referring to as the New Unionism. Lula and the metalworkers occupied a unique position on the left. They were creatures of trade unionism and industrial relations. They spoke in terms of open and fair negotiations over wages and work conditions, and so tended to ignore broad critiques of capitalism and foreign corporations. That orientation literally paid off for these workers. Foreign automobile executives often compared them to workers in North America's United Auto Workers and Germany's IG Metall union. Many throughout Brazilian society also saw them as distinct from the old populists and communists. Lula and other labor leaders moved to translate that popularity to the political system when they founded the PT in 1980.

The image of these unionists helped make the PT a national party whose leader contended for the presidency. As we have seen, Lula repeatedly came in second to the winner of three straight presidential elections. Despite the PT's status as neither populist nor communist, the former trade unionists were unable to reassure enough Brazilians that a Lula presidency would eschew radical politics for a more moderate social democratic perspective. The party's leaders understood this well by the late 1990s, and moderated their policy proposals to seem less threatening to business and the conservative sensibilities of many Brazilians of all social classes. Lula and other early party leaders were particularly sensitive to these issues in their home state of São Paulo. Lula's and the PT's history should have made them favorites in Brazil's richest and most populous state, but they failed to win there in the three presidential elections beginning in 1989. The party did win mayoral elections in the Paulista capital, but it could not win throughout the state.

São Paulo state is unique in Latin America. Its population, which was estimated in 2022 to be 46.7 million people, is only slightly less than that of Colombia (52 million), which is the third most populous Latin American nation behind Brazil (216 million) and Mexico (132 million). São Paulo is also an economic powerhouse with a highly productive modern agricultural sector dominated by coffee, sugar, soybeans, citrus fruits, and other commodities.

Brazil's automobile industry, banking, and other major industries are centered in the state, and it also has succeeded in merging its agricultural, commercial, and industrial sectors by becoming a leading producer of sugar-based ethanol. São Paulo's status as Brazil's most dynamic state has led its residents to refer to it as "the locomotive" of Brazil. In its more condescending version, Paulistas add that they are the locomotive pulling the 25 empty boxcars that are Brazil's other states. São Paulo's sense of itself was clear during the Old Republic when its governors traded the presidency with the governors of neighboring Minas Gerais. And the Old Republic came crashing down in 1930 when Paulista politicians insisted on keeping the presidency for two terms in a row. They further asserted their power and separateness in the 1932 Civil War.

Given the PT's roots in São Paulo's automobile industry, and the state's importance in national elections (it produces slightly more than one-fifth of the national vote total), Lula's failure to win there in three successive presidential elections revealed a few of the party's underlying weaknesses. Many among the state's large middle-class population worried about what they saw as the PT's radicalism. More significant was the fact that a growing number of São Paulo's poor were turning to evangelical Protestant churches, which preached very conservative politics. Although few political analysts understood the growing influence of the evangelical movement in the early 2000s, Lula and the PT were careful to present themselves as reformers who had not been involved in what was increasingly seen as a corrupt federal government. The party's refusal to enter into alliances with the other leading parties in the legislature ended up immunizing Lula and the PT from broad critiques of corruption in Brasília.

Going into 2002, Lula seemed to be the obvious choice to run under the PT banner, but various factions in the party challenged him given his three consecutive losses in 1989, 1994, and 1998. The party's left felt he had become too moderate, while others simply thought him unelectable. Lula easily prevailed in party voting, however, and became the PT candidate for October's polling. The challenges from within ended up strengthening him for the general election. Accusations from the left that he was too moderate served Lula well with the general electorate. There was also a push from some in the party to embrace specific social policies, such as an expansion of FHC's direct payments, and to make them into a basic income program for all Brazilians. Lula embraced parts of these programs, which appealed to the poor throughout the nation, particularly in the Northeast.

In the first round of voting on October 6, Lula had his best showing in such an open field, garnering 46.44% of the vote. The Paulista José Serra of the PMDB came in second with only 23.20%. Lula won the October 27 run-off with 61.27% of the vote, while Serra won only 38.73%. With that, Latin America's most populous nation, and the world's fourth most populous democracy (behind Indonesia, the United States, and India), elected to the presidency a former automobile worker and trade unionist who had left school when he was 14. When Lula took office on January 1, 2003, expectations among Brazilians and throughout the hemisphere were high. Unfortunately, his first challenge involved trying to work with one of Brazil's most important allies, the United States.

The George W. Bush administration had a decidedly negative and largely uninformed view of Lula and the PT. Political appointees in the Department of State and National Security Council denounced him as a socialist or worse, and grouped him with Venezuela's Hugo Chávez as an opponent. The Bush White House refused to send a high-level delegation to the inauguration, offering to have the US Trade Representative attend instead. Just days before the inauguration, members of the Brazilian media ambushed US Ambassador Donna Hrinak outside of a supermarket and demanded to know why her country hated Brazil's incoming president. She quipped that Americans love Lula because he went from the factory to the presidency, and that was an American-style success story. While Hrinak's charm and quick thinking put the matter to rest, it also foreshadowed what would become a fruitful relationship between Lula and Bush, and then Barack Obama. The socialist labor leader developed strong relations with successive American presidents because he governed pragmatically as a social democrat who promoted private enterprise and did not challenge the sanctity of property rights.

As president, Lula was quite moderate. He governed through a coalition with centrist and center-right parties, and was ultimately more of a reformer than anything else. His signature policy accomplishment was the Family Stipend (Bolsa Família), which dramatically decreased poverty throughout Brazil. The program provided a monthly wage to families whose children maintained high attendance records at school and were broadly vaccinated against disease through the public health service. School attendance increased with the Family Stipend in place, and child employment decreased accordingly. Independent analyses of income and social class in Brazil showed that by 2007, more than 23 million people categorized as the poorest in the nation moved from the lowest income categories into the lower middle class. Income inequality decreased by 20%, with no measurable drop in the wealth of those in the highest categories. The Family Stipend, along with an expanding economy, also led to significant increases in homeownership. In addition, Lula's administration implemented Zero Hunger (Fome Zero) to combat malnutrition. Like the Family Stipend, it focused on children. During his time in office, this program cut child hunger by 46%.

As successful as these programs were, they did not in any way undermine the economic status quo. In fact, they helped to spur domestic economic growth by dramatically expanding demand for

Brazilian-made goods and services. Lula's administration built new schools and health clinics to serve the expanding demand for education, vaccines, and other healthcare more broadly. That rising demand also led to expanded employment in the education and healthcare sectors. At the same time, Lula moved to reassure both foreign and domestic businesses that he would not fundamentally alter Brazil's economic system. He emphasized that he was a reformer whose social programs would strengthen capitalism through increased demand, and not a socialist who wanted to gain control over aspects of the private sector. Lula signaled this orientation at the start of his administration by placing centrists and conservatives with business ties in key government posts. He nominated Henrique Meirelles, who had been the head of Brazil's BankBoston branch and a PSDB politician, to be the chief of the Central Bank. The Meirelles appointment, and public statements agreeing to continue with International Monetary Fund agreements signed by the previous administration, affirmed Lula's position as a moderate on economic matters.

Lula's pragmatism led to a complex mix of policies. He was a moderate on macro-economic issues, but a progressive on social welfare with programs such as the Family Stipend. His administration was also forward-looking in the environmental realm. Since successive military regimes had turned to economic development in the Amazon region through road building and resettlement programs, Brazil had experienced such extensive levels of deforestation in order to bolster soybean production and cattle grazing that it garnered worldwide attention and frequent condemnation. Deforestation dates to the earliest days of European settlement. Much of the most productive coffee and soybean farms in the nation's Center-South region had once been part of an extensive Atlantic forest. But the highly mechanized and fast-moving deforestation of the Amazon region that began during the dictatorship did in only three decades more environmental damage than had been done over the course of the previous four centuries. Lula's government was the first to slow interior development to protect land, particularly for indigenous groups. Throughout his presidency, Lula worked to limit further deforestation and prosecute individuals who encroached on constitutionally protected indigenous land.

His government took a much more moderate or even conservative approach to foreign affairs. Lula built on the ties FHC had established, and continued to promote Brazil on the international stage. He even developed a close working relationship that some aides described as a real friendship with George W. Bush, whose administration had initially shunned him. Lula had a similar relationship with Venezuela's Hugo Chávez, demonstrating his pragmatism in international affairs. His visits to more than 80 nations promoted Brazilian exports and ideas, and made him a bit of a celebrity. All of this raised his and Brazil's stature on the world stage. Lula increasingly became a symbol of effective leadership from the Global South, and African and other nations sought out details of the Family Stipend, thinking they might adopt his administration's signature program. One result of his popularity and work on the world stage brought Brazil great international prestige, but ended up leaving many Brazilians discouraged about their nation's future. Lula and his team brought two mega-events to the country by securing the 2014 World Cup and 2016 Summer Olympics. The problems brought on by hosting these sports competitions would largely impact Lula's successor and close friend Dilma Rousseff.

Political Deal Making and Corruption

Not only did Lula appoint politicians from center and center-right parties to his cabinet, he also had to work closely with a wide variety of politicians from various parties to pass legislation. Like his predecessors, he did not have a governing majority in the legislature. The PT government, however, was caught going beyond simple horse trading and patronage to garner votes in the Chamber of Deputies and Senate. In mid-2005, a politician from the PTB went to the media to denounce the administration for paying legislators a monthly stipend of about US$12,000 in exchange for support of its programs. The scandal quickly became known as the *"mensalão"* or Monthly Allowance. Money for these payments was pulled from various

THE TRIUMPH OF SOCIAL DEMOCRACY (1994–2010) **163**

state enterprises, and went to legislators from a wide variety of center-right parties, including the PSDB, PTB, and PFL. Journalists uncovered payments, and government officials were caught with significant amounts of cash. A number of government officials from Lula's party resigned in disgrace, but no one could prove that Lula himself was involved in or even really knew about the payments.

Despite this broad scandal that had benefited his government by literally buying congressional support, Lula was reelected just a year later. Once again, in the first round in October 2006, he did quite well, winning just under 49% of the vote. This time, however, his main opponent, Geraldo Alckmin of the PSDB, was quite close to Lula in the first round with about 42% of the vote. Most commentators argued that Lula would have easily won the first round of voting had he not been saddled with the *mensalão* scandal. In the weeks before the October 19 run-off, Lula and Alckmin traded accusations about corruption. Alckmin had been a founding member of FHC's PSDB, and as such was open to accusations that he had at the very least been aware of similar vote-buying schemes during Cardoso's presidency. Whatever the facts about the two men's knowledge of or even participation in such payment schemes, however, corruption by both the PSDB and PT freed Lula from the full burden of the *mensalão*.

Lula ran on the success of the Family Stipend. He claimed that Alckmin and the PSDB would end the program if they took office. One way the PT supported claims about Alckmin and the PSDB was by focusing on the privatizations undertaken during the Cardoso years. Lula pointed out that the Vale do Rio Doce's profit each quarter was equal to the total price it had sold for back in 1997. That fact alone made the privatization seem corrupt, no matter how it had actually taken place. Lula then asked if Petrobras, the state-owned oil company founded by Vargas in 1953, was next. He and the PT sowed doubt about a possible PSDB government by detailing its close ties to business, and so implying that it would at least starve if not end the Family Stipend through corporate and other tax cuts and giveaways. This strategy worked brilliantly, and Lula crushed Alckmin in the second round of voting on October 29, receiving 61% of the vote to his opponent's 39%, three percentage points below his first round showing.

PT supporters and critics understood the importance of the Family Stipend to Lula's reelection. The only demographic group that Lula lost were those people with college degrees, and the only region he failed to win was the country's affluent Center-South. Lula and the PT crushed Alckmin in the Northeast with 76% of the region's votes. It was in this traditionally impoverished region where government support programs were dramatically improving most people's lives. The Center-South and South are also racially whiter than most of the rest of the nation, particularly the Northeast. To many Brazilians, the 2006 election reflected a growing racial and class divide, with critiques of the PT government often including racial narratives about buying the support of Brazil's large population of people of color in the Northeast and elsewhere. That sort of commentary steadily increased throughout Lula's second term, and would become prominent in the years that followed.

Lula left office at the end of the year in 2010, and turned power over to his hand-picked successor, Dilma Rousseff. Despite the *mensalão* scandal and other accusations of corruption, the PT government had presided over an era of economic stability and growth. The future also looked particularly bright. Lula had begun a program to pay for 100,000 Brazilian college graduates to go abroad for graduate study in the sciences. The Brazil Scientific Mobility Program was an investment in the future, and it was to be paid for with revenues from the massive deepwater oil deposits Petrobras discovered in 2006. Lula's administration forcefully argued that the coming oil money should not be squandered, and instead should be invested in science and industry to help catapult Brazil into the ranks of world economic leadership. In 2001, the investment bank Goldman Sachs had named Brazil one of the world's economies that would help determine the future of global growth. It was the "B" in BRIC. No matter what one makes of that designation decades later, it was part of a growing sense that perhaps the nation was finally achieving its true potential. It was no longer "the country of tomorrow."

Brazil had arrived. Sixteen years of political stability under Cardoso and Lula, a stable currency, continued growth, social and economic mobility, and plans for creating 100,000 new scientists were proof to many that Brazil had solved most of the long-term problems that had held it back for so long. And the world had noticed. Not only were Cardoso and Lula important figures in international affairs, the world was coming to Brazil for the World Cup and Summer Olympics. Brazilians and foreigners alike would see how far the nation had come, and how it had consigned to history the ugly legacy of military dictatorship and the economic and political disorder of the early years of the New Republic.

6

The Great Unraveling (2010–)

As the 2010 elections approached, Brazilians had a great deal to be thankful for. The nation had experienced 16 years of economic stability. The real was still the national currency, and hyperinflation seemed to be part of a distant history. The combination of Fernando Henrique Cardoso's neoliberalism, which was moderated by some protections for the poor, and Lula's expanded social programs, which depended on strong private sector growth, had improved most Brazilians' lives. It certainly made people confident about their futures in a way the country had not experienced since perhaps the 1960 opening of Brasília. The political system, although chaotic in practice and often tainted by corruption, was the most open and democratic in Brazil's history. When FHC handed the presidential sash to Lula on January 1, 2003, it was the first time a democratically elected president, who had served his entire electoral mandate (in this case, two four-year terms), turned over the office to another democratically elected president who would also serve out his terms in office.

There had been peaceful transfers of presidential power during the Old Republic, but the state governors and military men who served back then were not elected in anything resembling an open or democratic polity. And that was reflected in politics and policy. From the Empire through the Old Republic and Estado Novo, the focus of nearly all politics was an embrace of a form of economic liberalism. Especially after the 1888 abolition of slavery, Brazilian elites promoted and participated in a capitalist society that was well integrated in the world trading system. For most of its history, however, Brazil looked only to this aspect of liberalism. Political liberalism, with its associated freedoms, openness, and democratic elections, was largely absent. With the advent of the New Republic in 1985, but especially beginning with Cardoso's rise to the presidency, Brazil had finally succeeded in blending the economic and political components of liberalism. Brazilian and foreign commentators alike noted that Brazil in 2010 was 25 years beyond the dictatorship, and, like West Germany and Japan in 1970 (i.e. 25 years after the end of World War II), its democracy was well established and only growing stronger. The nation seemed to have finally put the political and economic instability of most of the twentieth century behind it as it entered the twenty-first.

Brazil's First Woman Leader Raises New Social Issues

Dilma Rousseff's presidential campaign seemed to be a triumph of Brazil's well-entrenched democratic norms, but in reality it was a warning sign that perhaps the system was not as robust as many believed. Dilma, as she is widely known, became the PT's presidential nominee for the 2010 election because Lula chose her, undermining the party's previous commitment to institutional democracy. She was an unlikely candidate for both personal and professional reasons. Dilma was the first woman nominated by a party with a strong chance to win the presidency, but her background as the PT candidate was more unique than her sex. Unlike Lula and most PT leaders, Dilma came from an elite background. A native of Minas Gerais, she was active in campus politics as a student, and then she joined part of the armed resistance to the dictatorship in the late 1960s. In the 1970s, she was arrested, jailed, and tortured by the military regime. She was frail and sickly when the military released her after two years of imprisonment. And then the Federal University of Minas Gerais used her arrest as a justification for expelling her just as she had recovered from torture and imprisonment.

In the early years of the New Republic, Dilma joined Leonel Brizola's Democratic Labor Party (PDT). It was not until 2000 that she left the PDT, which was closely associated with Brazil's old populist politics, and joined the PT. With Lula's support, she rose quickly through the party's ranks. Dilma was first the Minister of Energy (2003–5), which put her in charge of Petrobras and other key government agencies, and then the president's Chief of Staff (2005–10). In the middle of his second term in 2008, Lula publicly stated that he hoped a woman would head the PT ticket in 2010. That led many to believe that Marta Suplicy, a long-time PT member and former São Paulo mayor, would get the nod. Lula added her to his cabinet, and then she ran to return as mayor of Brazil's largest city. She lost that race, however, which undermined her presidential hopes, and inadvertently elevated Dilma among the PT leadership.

The party nominated Dilma, and then set about to make the usual alliances with other groups to create a winning coalition. The PT turned to the President of the Chamber of Deputies, Michel Temer of the PMDB, to run along with Dilma. Temer was a logical choice in terms of building a coalition, but he was also far to the PT's right politically. Before entering electoral politics, he had been a professor of constitutional law. Rousseff's and Temer's clearest challenge in the crowded first round of voting was the PSDB's José Serra, an American-trained economist who had served in Cardoso's cabinet and was the popular mayor of São Paulo. Serra's father had immigrated to Brazil from Italy. Temer's parents were both born in Lebanon, and Dilma's father came to Brazil from his home in Bulgaria. The immigrant parents of these three major figures in the 2010 election highlighted the complexity of ethnicity in Brazil. While about half of all Brazilians have some African heritage, the nation's Center-South has also been shaped by European immigration. Juscelino Kubitschek's (1956–61) Hungarian roots made him the first, and for some time the only, president of Brazil with non-Portuguese immigrant parents. The 2010 elections highlighted the diversity of Brazil's political class in the twenty-first century, although there was still no Afro-Brazilian representation at the top of the leading tickets.

Dilma and Temer came close to winning in the first round of voting with about 47%. Serra and his running mate, Indio da Costa, received 33% of the total. The Green Party ticket got 19.33%, but no other party even broke 1%. Dilma won the second round handily with 56% of the vote. The vote total reflected broad support for Lula's policies, and the hope that much would remain the same under Dilma. Moreover, policy makers and others believed that Brazil's recent offshore oil discoveries would easily fund expanded social spending. Production in the so-called pre-salt oil fields became a perfect metaphor for Brazil at this time. Experts agreed that it was one of the largest finds in decades, but they also warned that the location of the bulk of the oil – deep below the seabed in the layer before salt – would make removing it technologically challenging and expensive.

In 2006, Petrobras announced the massive find in the Santos Basin, which is about 300 km southeast of the Paulista port of Santos. The company began production two years later. Petrobras quickly removed the most accessible oil, and then had to plan to drill under the salt layer, more than 6,000 m below the seabed. In addition to the challenges of drilling at such great depths, the salt layer also made it particularly difficult to bring out the oil. Near the end of Lula's second term, the government introduced the Pre-Salt Law to address how the nation would maintain control over what it saw as a key to its economic future. The law created production sharing agreements between Petrobras and other companies, rather than complete concessions to foreign firms. The government also encouraged foreign oil services firms to develop their technologies for pre-salt extraction in collaboration with Brazilian companies. Lula's administration was addressing a key issue for Brazil. So much of the nation's history revolved around the production and export of commodities. In the early to mid-twentieth century, military leaders, industrialists, modernist intellectuals, and policy makers had increasingly worried about the effect that this dependence on exports would have on national development. Starting with Vargas, and continuing with the Kubitschek administration and military dictatorship, the state worked to diversify the economy. Lula's idea was to connect commodity production to further industrial growth through the manufacture of advanced drilling and other equipment. That would be achieved via partnerships with foreign firms, which included technology transfers, rather than concessions to outside companies that would make no long-lasting investments in Brazil.

The promise of ever-expanding oil revenue, along with the prestige of hosting the 2014 World Cup and then the 2016 Summer Olympics, added to Dilma's and the PT's popularity. Brazil seemed to be a leader on the world stage, and the coming oil revenue would guarantee that it could continue to fund the Family Stipend and other social programs. The Brazilian government seemed to be thinking strategically by leveraging the massive oil find with requirements that production in the Santos Basin would also encourage further national development of oil services and other related industries. In this atmosphere of hopefulness, Dilma moved to address one of Brazil's most enduring problems: racial bigotry. In August 2012, the president signed a broad affirmative action measure known as the Law of Social Quotas. The legislature passed the bill nearly unanimously. Just before the vote, in April 2012, the Supreme Court had unanimously upheld affirmative action quotas in higher education. The court ruling and new law seemed to indicate broad support for addressing the ways race had helped to make Brazil one of the world's most unequal societies.

From the outside, Lula's and Dilma's legislative achievements seemed to indicate broad support for progressive policies and social welfare spending. The PT governments' successes, however, were due more to a complex set of political alliances than to broad ideological agreement. Since at least the Cardoso years, but especially under Lula and Dilma, presidents have only succeeded legislatively by compromising with a group of politicians who make up what is known in Brazil as the *Centrão*, or the Big Center. Although the name implies that the politicians in this group are moderates who make up the center, they really are just a rump group without any clear ideology. They instead have a rock-solid commitment to maintaining their presence in the legislature through the use of broad patronage. Given the presence of more than 30 political parties, about half of which have a presence in the Chamber of Deputies, Cardoso, Lula, and Dilma all had to rely on making deals with members of the *Centrão* to advance their legislative agendas. The *mensalão* scandal during Lula's administration was one of the rare moments when this sort of deal making became public.

The Judiciary Enters Politics

A seemingly obscure judicial investigation quickly undermined the national sense of economic and social progress that had begun under FHC, and grew dramatically during Lula's and Dilma's PT administrations. Investigators uncovered the ways the revenue being generated by the massive petroleum projects in the Santos Basin was being used in a new bribery scheme that seemed bigger and broader than any previous episodes of corruption. It had begun in March 2014 as an investigation of money laundering through small businesses, such as gas stations and car washes. The investigators assigned it the code name Operation Car Wash (*Operação Lava Jato*). It quickly ballooned into one of the biggest international bribery scandals ever uncovered, with an estimated $5 billion in bribes and kickbacks. It primarily involved Petrobras overpaying for oil services and other contracts, and then having some of the money sent back to various politicians.

The Car Wash investigations had long-term repercussions for Brazilian politics, and ultimately were themselves a form of corruption. But when the federal police made the first arrests, it seemed as though an important missing piece of Brazil's political development had been finally been found. An apparently independent judiciary, in this case under the leadership of Judge Sérgio Moro, had uncovered and prosecuted corruption by some of the most powerful politicians in the country. The government was absent in the investigations of Fernando Collor de Mello. A combination of media investigations and his brother's denunciation had led to his impeachment. Allegations about corruption under Fernando Henrique Cardoso and the *mensalão* scandal during Lula's administration had, likewise, been uncovered by journalists. Car Wash was the product of aggressive and seemingly independent government investigators. And it relied on a major anti-corruption statute Dilma had signed into law in 2013.

Although news about the Car Wash investigations filled the airwaves, Dilma campaigned on the PT's many achievements over the last 12 years as the 2014 elections loomed. The growing scandal did, however, erode her popularity. She faced another crowded field, but one led by Tancredo Neves's grandson, Aécio

Neves of the PSDB. Dilma bested him by 42–35% in the first round of voting, and won in the second round 51.65–48.35%. The closeness of the vote reflected growing popular discontent with ongoing PT governance, and the sense that Dilma was a weak leader. In an environment of personalistic politics, she remained more of a stand-in for Lula than anything else, and that would ultimately undermine her popularity and power. Given her weak personal powerbase, growing popular anger about the Car Wash investigations left her in a tenuous position when broad protests against rising fuel costs gripped the nation early in her second term. Increased prices, just as the nation was celebrating its massive oil deposits, not only affected middle-class and working-class car owners, but they also drove up the cost of public transportation.

Working-class and poor Brazilians next protested against the poor quality of public health services throughout the nation. The broad complaints about the under-funded public health service represented a new challenge for the government. Lula and Dilma had long touted the PT's record in providing expanded services to the populace, and public health clinics and schools were the most common points of contact for the majority of Brazilians and their government. This was especially true for the PT's base because so many upper-middle-class and wealthy Brazilians used private doctors and sent their children to private schools. Like the developing Car Wash scandal, discontent over public health services undermined what the PT had argued they had done to push forward national progress. Oil revenue seemed to be doing more to line politicians' pockets than deepen development, and the great growth in federal spending had not yet made something as basic as public health work for the bulk of the population.

The public mood continued to sour with every new revelation from the Car Wash investigation. The Brazilian-based multinational construction company Odebrecht played a central role in the kickbacks in Brazil and other countries. Although neither Lula nor Dilma was directly implicated at first, the far-ranging investigation would, as we shall see, eventually lead in 2016–17 to Lula's arrest and conviction in such a controversial manner that the former president was considered a political prisoner by the United Nations. Before then, the broad popular mood had soured on the PT and most politicians. The fact that Dilma had had oversight of Petrobras while serving in Lula's cabinet increased popular distrust of the president. In this environment, Sérgio Moro and his investigators seemed to be the only heroes in the Brazilian polity, and their work appeared to indicate that the judiciary had finally established itself as an important institution in Brazil's democratic system.

Dilma began her second term politically weakened, and she never recovered. Right after the second round of voting was completed, Aécio Neves contested the results. He demanded a thorough recount, which confirmed that he had lost, but his initial refusal to accept defeat undermined Dilma's legitimacy among some Brazilians. It was in this political environment that the PMDB chose to abandon its alliance with the PT, putting the vice president, Michel Temer, in opposition to the president. The PT's standing declined with each new Car Wash revelation, even those about politicians from other parties. Dilma, who had never had the sort of personal popularity of Lula or even FHC, saw her approval ratings drop steadily throughout this period. She became the face of corruption, even though there were no credible accusations that she had participated in the kickback scheme.

When Vice President Temer abandoned the coalition, conservative opponents in the legislature moved against Dilma. They initiated impeachment proceedings, but they did so without a clear idea of exactly what impeachable acts she had committed. That did not deter her opponents. Legislators crafted an indictment around Dilma's use of a budgeting procedure that had been widely used by her predecessors, but was not technically appropriate. The flimsiness of the charges were beside the point. With 69 seats, the PT had more representatives in the Chamber of Deputies than any other party, but that was a tiny minority of the 513 total. The party had the second most senators with 12, but that too was a minority of the 81 total. The PMDB had a significant number of legislators, but had recently pulled out of the coalition government. From the start of the process in December 2015 through to its end, Dilma's opponents openly, even gleefully, spoke in openly sexist terms. Her opponents did not focus on her alleged wrongdoing. It was simply a matter of the PMDB taking the presidency from the PT. In addition to the open sexism, her opponents publicly discussed undoing the recently passed affirmative action law. And so conservatives openly celebrated their ability to bring down the leftist government, and on August 31, 2016, the Senate voted 61–20 to find Dilma guilty of violating budgeting laws and to remove her from office.

Michel Temer had begun serving as Brazil's interim president on May 12 as the impeachment was proceeding. He immediately staked out his position as a conservative interested in reducing social spending, claiming somewhat farcically that slashing spending and so aggregate demand would jumpstart the economy. He called for cutting funding for public health and education, which had grown through the Family Stipend. Temer achieved this by forcing through a constitutional amendment restricting growth in the budget to the previous year's rate of inflation. This completely reversed years of effective social spending that had begun under Cardoso in the 1990s and early 2000s, and was accelerated by Lula and Dilma. The amendment allowed legislators to avoid direct votes cutting spending, especially on popular programs such as public health and education, and set spending limits in place until it could be removed from the constitution.

Temer succeeded in the short term, but his tenure was brief. He and many of his allies were more corrupt than they had (groundlessly) accused Dilma of being. Politicians and businessmen were caught openly discussing bribes they had paid to Temer. The media had tapes of Temer as president discussing making hush money payments to people who had threatened to go public with details of his corruption. In June 1917, less than one year after Dilma was forced out of office, he was criminally charged. In March 2020, he was arrested as part of the ongoing Car Wash investigations. It was perhaps this scandal that led the PMDB to rebrand itself as the MDB, its original name during the *Abertura*.

A Tainted Election Shakes the Nation

The 2018 general election was set to take place in this environment of broad distrust of and unhappiness with politicians. But Lula remained broadly popular. Despite the *mensalão* scandal and the fact that so many in the PT were implicated by Car Wash, he seemed to be above the fray. The constitution also did not prohibit more than two terms in office as president, so long as these were not served consecutively. Before Lula could begin to campaign, however, and just after Dilma was removed from office, Sérgio Moro filed money laundering charges against him in September 2016. Moro charged the former president with nine separate crimes, but he was only convicted of one. He was found guilty of accepting an extensive renovation on a condominium that he allegedly owned in a beach town in the state of São Paulo. Throughout the trial, Lula's attorneys argued that he did not actually own the property, and prosecutors could not locate records demonstrating that he did.

In July 2017, Moro personally sentenced Lula to nine and a half years' imprisonment. An appeals court affirmed his conviction and increased his sentence to 12 years in January 2018. That April, Lula lost his final appeal and was ordered to prison. In June 2019, however, the media outlet *The Intercept* received secretly recorded audio in which Moro and others discussed investigating, indicting, and trying Lula explicitly to keep him from running for president in 2018. National and international reaction was swift. Foreign governments openly referred to Lula as a political prisoner. The evidence and the pressure were so powerful that the Supreme Federal Court annulled Lula's conviction and ordered him released from prison. But the damage had already been done and Moro and others had succeeded in keeping Lula from running in the 2018 election, which helped an obscure right-wing politician become president during a dangerous time in the nation's and world's history.

Jair Bolsonaro had a long, but not particularly distinguished, career in the Chamber of Deputies. He represented part of Rio de Janeiro from 1991 through the 2018 presidential campaign. Before politics, Bolsonaro had served in the army, attaining the rank of captain. Throughout his adult life, he has remained a cheerleader for the military and continues to speak favorably of the 1964–85 dictatorship. Bolsonaro even chose a retired general, Hamilton Maurão, as his running mate. He campaigned as an outsider and savior of the nation, and he presented himself as a strongman who could bring order to the chaotic political environment ushered in by the Car Wash investigations. Bolsonaro ran as the candidate of the Liberal Social Party (Partido Liberal Social, PLS), but that was just a formality. He and Maurão ran as mavericks who were not tied to the old politics.

Bolsonaro is a practicing Catholic, but Michele de Paula Bolsonaro, his third wife, whom he married in 2007, is an Evangelical Christian. There are even credible reports that Jair Bolsonaro was also baptized as an evangelical. Whatever the truth about his religious practices, his wife's close association with the fastest-growing religious group in Brazil provided a great deal of political support for his campaign. Bolsonaro is also widely recognized as the first presidential candidate to successfully leverage social media in a Brazilian election. His campaign was particularly adroit in deploying WhatsApp to spread misinformation about his opponents and mobilize his supporters. They went so far as to send messages out to the 120 million Brazilian users of the app providing the voting number 17 with Lula's name. This was a way to confuse some Brazilians into voting for Bolsonaro, who had been assigned number 17 on the ballot. It was just one of many examples of misinformation pushed out by the Bolsonaro campaign.

Bolsonaro's ties to the evangelical community and his campaign's deft use of social media combined to propel him forward after he survived an assassination attempt during a September 2018 campaign stop in Minas Gerais. A man later determined by the courts to be criminally insane attacked Bolsonaro with a knife. After the candidate's family initially downplayed the severity of his wounds, he was transferred to Brazil's premier medical facility, São Paulo's Albert Einstein Jewish Hospital, where he recuperated for about a month. All of his opponents condemned the attack, and the police found that his assailant had acted alone. Bolsonaro's status as a victim of political violence and his frequent invocations of bible verses to describe his struggle and state of mind meanwhile elevated his candidacy in the eyes of many.

The election became a contest between an institutional stalwart representing a movement, the PT's Fernando Haddad, and an outspoken nonconformist in Bolsonaro. Haddad is a São Paulo-based academic with a masters in Economics and a doctorate in Philosophy. Throughout his career, he combined his work at the University of São Paulo with public service. Haddad served as the Minister of Education under both Lula and Dilma, following that service with his election as mayor of São Paulo. He took office on January 1, 2013, and almost immediately had to deal with massive public protests over increases in the cost of public transportation. Despite growing dissatisfaction with his mayoralty, he was the most logical option for the PT after Moro had Lula jailed. Bolsonaro had a large plurality of the first round voting with 46% of the total; Haddad received 29%. Bolsonaro then easily won the run-off with 55% of the vote.

Bolsonaro wasted little time in moving policy to the far right, especially on environmental issues. The new president signaled his government's desire to expand development throughout the Amazon region, no matter how that would trample the constitutionally protected rights of indigenous Brazilians or further denigrate the environment. He channeled the ugly sexism of Dilma's impeachment, and openly argued that women should not be considered men's equals. Bolsonaro argued that that meant women should be paid less than men for the same work. He was also aggressively homophobic, and even endorsed some violence against Brazil's LGBTQ+ community. Those calls fit in with Bolsonaro's general support for political violence against his real and perceived opponents. His pronouncements led some in the Brazilian and US-based media to label him the "Tropical Trump" because he shared the crude and violent political style of the then American president. Bolsonaro and his family (one of his sons is a Federal Deputy) visited Donald Trump at his Florida resort, and the Brazilian president did all in his power to emulate his American counterpart.

Bolsonaro continued to mimic the American president when he, too, tried to downplay the severity of the growing Covid-19 pandemic in 2020. He embraced crackpot cures and denigrated mask-wearing, vaccinations, and other science-based measures to mitigate illness. Not surprisingly, after the first full year of the pandemic in April 2021, Brazil had the highest Covid death rate in the world. In addition to being overrun with desperately sick patients, hospitals in some large cities completely ran out oxygen for people in their intensive care units. Bolsonaro's gross mishandling of the pandemic response, along with the already problematic nature of Brazil's underfunded public health system, eroded the president's popularity. Even before the pandemic, he had done little to generate confidence that he could shepherd the Brazilian economy in any environment. As Covid took its toll, Bolsonaro's many weaknesses further undermined the nation's ability to navigate through such challenging times.

Brazil Embraces Democracy, Again

Bolsonaro signaled his political weaknesses when he repeatedly refused to say he would accept the results of the 2022 presidential election. He continued to cultivate the military's leadership, and hinted that they would assist him in preventing his political opponents from taking office if they prevailed in the October elections. That election would reveal all the ways Brazil's democratic system was much weaker than so many people had assumed. Lula's decision to run, and his immediate status as the frontrunner against an incumbent, called into question Bolsonaro's 2018 victory because he won against a weak PT candidate. The politically motivated jailing of Lula before the 2018 election had prevented the frontrunner from standing for office. For close to a year in 2022, Lula and Bolsonaro ignored all the other politicians who announced they might run, including Sérgio Moro, and attacked each other over their obvious policy differences. Although most polls indicated that Lula was so popular that he could receive more than half the vote in the first round held on October 2, the final tally was much closer than most observers had expected. Lula received 48.4% of the total, and Bolsonaro 43.2%. Bolsonaro and his supporters immediately assailed the polls and much of the political press as biased against them.

Not only did Bolsonaro do better in the first round of voting than the pollsters thought he would, but candidates associated with him through the Liberal Party (Partido Liberal or PL) did as well. The PL not only gained congressional seats, it also won in many state and municipal elections. Although the party existed long before Bolsonaro rose to prominence, and it is considered part of the *Centrão*, in 2022 it was increasingly tied to the controversial president. The PL's electoral success revealed the breadth and depth of opposition to the PT and its allies on the left and in the political center.

Despite having broad support from many in the business community, Bolsonaro continued to present himself as an outsider fighting against a corrupt establishment. His authoritarian bent, along with his bungled response to the Covid pandemic, did, however, lead a great many in Brazil's political establishment to coalesce around Lula's candidacy. This process began when the centrist former governor of São Paulo, Geraldo Alckmin, left the PSDB to join the more leftist Socialist Party (PSB, Partido Socialista Brasileiro) to be Lula's running mate. A steady stream of PSDB and MDB political figures followed and embraced Lula. Fernando Henrique Cardoso, who had loudly opposed previous PT governments, openly embraced Lula as the champion of Brazilian democracy, and then campaigned in public with him.

Bolsonaro's allies in the Federal Police were caught attempting to suppress the vote in heavily pro-Lula parts of the Northeast. The Federal Election Chief had to intervene with the police to end roadblocks and other tactics they were using to keep people from their polling stations. The Election Chief guaranteed the public during the ongoing voting that the illegal police tactics had done more to delay than to prevent people from getting to the polls. Voting and vote counting moved quickly because Brazil only uses electronic voting, and the results were available just hours after the polls closed. Lula won with 50.9% of the vote to Bolsonaro's 49.1%. Lula received 60,345,999 votes (of 118,552,353 ballots cast) for a 1.8% margin.

Although a close result, Lula defeated the incumbent president, and he did so in the name of returning the Brazilian political system to the path it had entered on in 1985 at the end of the 21-year military dictatorship. With the announcement of his victory, Lula tweeted simply "*democracia*." World leaders quickly noted the outcome in order to promote stability and political peace. US President Joe Biden and French President Emmanuel Macron did so publicly. The Chinese and Russian foreign ministries followed later that day.

Bolsonaro remained silent for close to 48 hours after his loss had become apparent. On the Tuesday after Sunday's vote, thousands of his supporters took to Brazil's highways to demand he stay in office, or that the military stage a coup. Truckers blocked about 270 federal highways in 13 states, tying up traffic in Brazil's most-populated areas as a show of force. They burned tires and other debris. Federal authorities threatened the truckers with arrest and significant fines if they did not move. The government then began the process of forcibly opening the highways. Just as authorities worked to disperse the protesters, Bolsonaro finally appeared in public to discuss the election. Without admitting defeat, he said that he would follow the constitution and work to promote a smooth transition to a new administration. In his very brief remarks, the outgoing president noted, "The right has truly emerged in our country. Our robust representation in Congress shows the strength of our values: God, country, family, and freedom."

Back to Brazil's Future

When Lula appeared in public soon after the vote totals were announced, he spoke at length about ending the deforestation of the Amazon region, eradicating hunger in the world's third largest food producer, and bringing Brazilians together after four years of bruising divisions. Lula said, in part, "I will govern for the 215 million Brazilians . . . and not just those who voted for me. There are not two Brazils. We are one country, one people, a great nation." But the nation seems more divided today than at any point since the 1964 military coup. Bolsonaro narrowly lost, but his allies in congressional and gubernatorial elections did well. PL candidates took a plurality of seats in the Chamber of Deputies and will serve as governors of eight of Brazil's 26 states, including São Paulo and Rio de Janeiro. The right's electoral strength, despite the many problems of the Bolsonaro administration, points to a deep political divide. That divide, combined with the weak hand Brazilian presidents have had in dealing with the legislature since the late 1980s, will make the incoming president's job that much harder.

Lula's assertion that "there are not two Brazils" speaks directly to the nation's long history of incomplete state making and national development. For most of its history, Brazil has been defined by a series of binaries. By the time the Portuguese crown arrived in 1808, Brazil was slave and free, coastal and interior, urban and rural, and those divides shaped politics and society throughout the nineteenth century and beyond. Many nations have faced similar situations. The United States is the Western Hemisphere's most obvious example from its Civil War to the ongoing divisions between so-called Blue and Red states. One of the things that makes Brazil somewhat unique, however, is the ways it has addressed those issues. Faith in a series of national myths about being a racial democracy, not being as violent as other Latin American nations, and being the country of the future has shaped how Brazilian political and other leaders have made policy and acted.

From the 1822 *Grito de Ipiranga* to the November 1889 declaration of the Republic through the Revolution of 1930 and the 1964 military coup, the most significant events in the nation's history have not included the broad participation of the Brazilian people or discourses of popular democracy. Paradoxically, the 21-year military dictatorship changed that. Brazilians developed strong ideas of what a functioning democracy should be: it should be the opposite of the dictatorship they were living through. Over the course of the *Abertura* and the early years of the New Republic, Brazilians put in place a new constitution that dramatically broadened popular participation in the system. Then, over the course of two decades of governance by Fernando Henrique Cardoso, Luiz Inácio Lula da Silva, and Dilma Rousseff from 1995 to 2016, Brazil seemed to have finally developed a highly effective, if flawed, democratic system that simultaneously promoted ongoing capitalist development and new levels of social justice and broad wellbeing. Poverty, hunger, and homelessness did not disappear, but they did shrink considerably during those two decades.

Jair Bolsonaro's 2018 election and his four years in office shocked many in Brazil and beyond. He won in part because a corrupt group of prosecutors and judges had jailed Lula, who was handily beating him in the polls. Bolsonaro's campaign also relied on the deliberate and broad dissemination of misinformation. In office, he denigrated women, members of the LBGTQ+ communities, and anyone else with whom he disagreed. He was also broadly incompetent, which became obvious as the Covid-19 pandemic grew. By mid-October 2022, Brazil had suffered the second highest number of Covid-19 deaths (687,680) in the world, second only to the United States (1,092,948). But Bolsonaro was not an outlier or political fluke. He represents a potent conservative movement that rejects the political, social, and economic progress made in the years since 1985. The publicly stated nostalgia for the military dictatorship among his supporters made that obvious, but the 2016 impeachment of Dilma Rousseff should have been understood as foreshadowing the rise of Bolsonaro or someone like him. The weak party system and prevalence of personalist politics led her vice president, Michel Temer, to quit the coalition and lead the charge against her. Rousseff was impeached because her opponents could take power, not because she had violated the law.

The impeachment proceedings revealed much that was wrong with Brazil, from the disgusting public displays of misogyny to the cavalier use of impeachment itself to grab power. The 1992 Collor de Mello impeachment, although based on real crimes, also exposed significant dysfunction within the system. The success of the FHC and Lula years simply obscured many of those issues. But even with those obvious problems in the political system, Brazil had finally made great progress addressing many of its long-term challenges. In its second century of independence, it diversified its economy so much so that it ranks third in agricultural output worldwide and fifth in total agricultural exports by value, and at the same time is the fourteenth largest manufacturing nation. Highways connect most of the country, which is also well served by a complex system of cellular telephony supported by Brazil's own telecommunications satellites controlled by the Brazilian Space Agency (AEB, Agência Espacial Brasileira). And the nation is governed from its modernist interior capital, Brasília. Brazilians, through dictatorship and democracy, have done a great deal to tie together the nation economically, politically, and socially and so have begun to diminish its many dichotomies. Lula, though, would not have had to declare "there are not two Brazils" upon winning the 2022 presidential election if it were true. His declaration remains more of an aspiration than a fact. Going forward, the question will be if Brazil can continue to make progress toward that goal, or if it will remain an incomplete project of nation building.

Afterword

On January 8, 2023, a pro-Bolsonaro mob attacked all three branches of Brazil's government in Brasília's Three Powers Plaza. Dressed in green and yellow shirts, often in the Brazilian national team's kit, the rioters trashed portions of the Planalto Presidential Palace, Supreme Federal Court, and National Congress building. They smashed windows, destroyed furniture (including Juscelino Kubitschek's desk), and slashed paintings throughout all three buildings. For hours, they roamed the Three Powers Plaza after overwhelming the meager security presence. The rioters also targeted journalists whom they blamed for supporting Lula in what they claimed was a stolen election. None of the branches of government was in session, and Lula was in São Paulo state at the time of the unrest. The rioters may have chosen to act when Brasília was relatively empty to take advantage of the limited security presence, but there is also evidence that the Federal District's governor and members of the police and military knew of the attack in advance, and did nothing to stop it. Indeed, there is video of police officers mingling around the mob during the attack.

The January 8 Brasília riot was not an isolated event. On December 12, 2022, the day the Superior Electoral

Court ratified Lula's electoral victory, Bolsonaro supporters attacked the Federal Police headquarters in Brasília. They burned cars on the streets, and had to be subdued by the security forces. Police uncovered a plan to bomb portions of the Brasília International Airport on December 23. Violence and attacks on the nation's infrastructure continued after the Brasília riot. On January 9, there were attempts to disable the power grids in Paraná and Rondônia, two pro-Bolsonaro states. Soon after those incidents, someone used a tractor to try to demolish a transmission tower from the giant Itaipú Dam. There were also attacks on parts of the grid in the interior of São Paulo state.

It is not hard to see clear connections to the January 6, 2021, storming of the US Capitol. Bolsonaro became a close Trump ally, and several of the former American president's confidants had spent time in Brazil advising their South American counterparts. One of Bolsonaro's sons, Eduardo, had talked to a number of people involved in the attack in Washington. Journalists reported that his primary take-away was that Trump had erred in relying on the rioters. The Bolsonaros sought institutional support through the military and police for their coup attempt. Nevertheless, despite receiving some significant assistance from people in those institutions, it was not enough to sustain the insurrection beyond the hours of the attack on the Three Powers Plaza.

The riot changed everything about Lula's first weeks back in office, and presented new challenges and opportunities for the incoming president and Brazilian democracy. Many of Bolsonaro's supporters, refusing to accept Lula's victory, had been camping near military bases trying to convince the Army to act and remove the democratically elected president, or even prevent him from being sworn in. They were not a disorganized mob. They had funding from large agribusinesses and other private sector interests. Their encampments were comfortable and stocked with a steady supply of food and other amenities. Some military and police officials also seem to have protected them before the riot, and then prevented federal authorities from arresting them after.

Upon taking office on January 1, 2023, Lula already faced a series of daunting problems. Like all of his predecessors in the post-1985 period, the newly sworn-in president would have to find ways to pass legislation in a fragmented and increasingly polarized legislature. Although Lula had defeated Bolsonaro for the presidency, he did so narrowly. Moreover, far-right supporters of the former president expanded their presence in both houses of the Congress. In that precarious environment, Lula also had to deal with the lingering effects of the Covid-19 pandemic, as well as a shaky economy facing both high inflation and the prospects of a recession throughout the industrialized world. During his first administration, Lula had benefited from a robust economy marked by high commodity prices that allowed him to fund his ambitious agenda. Conditions in 2023, along with the highly polarized political situation at home, presented new and seemingly intractable challenges.

Lula's closest advisors, including Finance Minister Fernando Haddad, have spoken of the riots as a policy inflection point. Haddad said that the new PT administration would perhaps focus on increasing taxes on the wealthy in order to pay for social and environmental programs. Implicit in the comments he made at Davos in mid-January 2023 was the idea that there was broad popular support for making many of the real and perceived Bolsonaro supporters literally pay for the PT's policy agenda. Lula himself began the process of building a broad political consensus against those he and most Brazilians see as challenging the nation's democracy. He explicitly ordered the military to follow its constitutional duty supporting democracy, and to avoid undermining it: "The armed forces have a defined role under the constitution which is the defense of the Brazilian people and the defense of our sovereignty against external conflicts. That's what I want them to do." He has also continued to back his conservative Defense Minister, José Múcio. Although far to Lula's right, he is close to the president. Lula is leveraging that relationship to demonstrate to the more rational members of the military his desire to work with all supporters of Brazil's constitution no matter what their politics are.

The president deepened this pro-democracy coalition by bringing together the nation's governors (excluding Ibaneis Rocha of the Federal District, who was suspended for 90 days by the Justice of the Supreme Court Alexandre de Moraes) for a tour of the damage done in Brasília. The national media were on hand to record Lula and the governors as they reviewed the destruction throughout the Three Powers Plaza. Their presence together sent a strong national message of unity and support for democracy. It also signaled Lula's shrewd use of one the political system's most obvious weaknesses – the tendency for personalism – to his advantage. The rioters and Bolsonaro himself were not part of an institution that could publicly support them. Unlike in the United States, where the Republican Party and its media allies have tried to whitewash the January 6 insurrection at the Capitol, the Brazilian right is highly fragmented around a number of individual politicians who see no advantage in associating themselves with the January 8 rioters.

It is impossible to know how events will unfold as Brasília moves from the immediate aftermath of the attack to the business of governing. Just as it has since the establishment of the Republic in 1889, the military continues to play an outsized role in determining the nation's future. But, beyond that fact, and the uniqueness of Bolsonaro and his desire to emulate a disgraced former US president, January 8 in Brazil highlights a key tension in the nation's history between a tendency toward authoritarianism and the struggle to establish a robust functioning democracy. Lula, both as Brazil's president and as a symbol of popular democracy, faces a complex struggle against a wide array of entrenched and powerful anti-democratic forces. As a political leader who entered the national stage during the *Abertura* and who worked assiduously to build real democratic institutions in Brazil, he may be the ideal figure to defend and promote the 1988 constitution. If he succeeds, Brazil could become a potent example of the resilience of democratic norms in a world where illiberal politics seem to be on the march. If Lula and the political establishment fail, however, Brazil could remain stuck in a state of incompleteness, with authoritarian and democratic forces each struggling to define the nation.

Further Reading

There is a terrific and growing literature on modern Brazilian history. I have included here works in English by both Brazilian and foreign authors. There are wonderful histories that are only available in Portuguese that should be consulted by anyone who reads the language, and wants to know well the nation's past. Although this book does not cover the colonial period, works by Brazil's first professional historians have influenced my analysis of the nation's modern history. João Capistrano de Abreu's *Chapters of Brazil's Colonial History, 1500–1800* (New York: Oxford University Press, 1997 [1907]), while focused on Brazil's colonial past, sets out the key issue of how the nation has struggled to gain control over its massive national territory, and how that has shaped its economic, social, and political scene from the sixteenth century forward. Sérgio Buarque de Holanda's *Roots of Brazil* (South Bend, IN: Notre Dame University Press, 2012 [1936]) connects the European, indigenous, and African origins of Brazilian society to paint a complex picture of a new world in the tropics.

Independence and early nation making in Brazil were different from the rest of Latin America. Roderick J. Barman's *Brazil: The Forging of a Nation, 1789–1852*

(Stanford: Stanford University Press, 1988) provides a careful study of how the move to independence and the politics of the early Empire did not lead to the fracturing of Portuguese America into multiple nations, along the lines of Spanish America. Jeffrey D. Needell analyzes high politics in the early Empire in *The Politics of Order: The Conservatives, the State, and Slavery in the Brazilian Monarchy, 1831–1871* (Stanford: Stanford University Press, 2006). Judy Bieber's *Power, Patronage, and Political Violence: State Building on a Brazilian Frontier, 1822–1889* (Lincoln: University of Nebraska Press, 1999) moves the analysis away from Rio and other central areas to more peripheral regions to understand politics during the Empire.

Studies of slavery in Brazil are among the best works on unfree labor for anywhere in the world. A pioneering study of early coffee production under slavery is Stanley J. Stein's *Vassouras: A Coffee County, 1850–1900. The Roles of Planter and Slave in a Plantation Society* (Princeton: Princeton University Press, 1985 [1957]). Emília Viotta da Costa's *The Brazilian Empire: Myths and Histories* (Chicago: University of Chicago Press, 1985) does a masterful job of connecting slavery to broader issues in Brazilian society, as well as comparing land tenure and labor in Brazil and the United States. The complexities of race and gender in urban slavery are well detailed in Sandra Lauderdale Graham's *House and Street: The Domestic World of Servants and Masters in Nineteenth-Century Rio de Janeiro* (Cambridge: Cambridge University Press,

1988). The single best work on the abolitionist movement is Celso Thomas Castilho's *Slave Emancipation and Transformations in Brazilian Citizenship* (Pittsburgh: University of Pittsburgh Press, 2016).

Politics during the Empire in general is well studied by Richard Graham in his *Patronage and Politics in Nineteenth-Century Brazil* (Stanford: Stanford University Press, 1990), while the later period is captured well by Moritz Schwarcz's *The Emperor's Beard: Dom Pedro II and the Tropical Monarchy of Brazil* (New York: Hill & Wang, 2004) and Roderick J. Barman's *Citizen Emperor: Pedro II of Brazil* (Cambridge: Cambridge University Press, 1999). Popular politics is analyzed in Yuko Miki's *Frontiers of Citizenship: A Black and Indigenous History of Postcolonial Brazil* (Cambridge: Cambridge University Press, 2018).

The culture and politics of the Old Republic are deftly explored by Jeffrey D. Needell's *A Tropical Belle Époque: Elite Culture and Society in Turn-of-the-Century Rio de Janeiro* (Cambridge: Cambridge University Press, 1987). José Murilo de Carvalho's *The Formation of Souls: Imagery of the Republic in Brazil* (South Bend, IN: Notre Dame University Press, 2012) details the rise of nationalist tropes in the Old Republic. Popular rejection of the Old Republic in the countryside is brilliantly chronicled by Todd A. Diacon in *Millenarian Vision, Capitalist Reality: Brazil's Contestado Rebellion, 1912–1916* (Durham, NC: Duke University Press, 1991). The economy of this period is comprehensively covered in Steve Topik's *The Political Economy of the Brazilian State, 1889–1930* (Austin: University of Texas Press, 1987). Mauricio Font's *Coffee and Transformation in São Paulo, Brazil* (Lanham, MD: Lexington Books, 2010) analyzes the impact of coffee on broad economic development.

Although not as extensively studied as race and slavery, immigration and ethnicity are central issues for Brazilian history. Jeffrey Lesser's *Immigration, Ethnicity, and National Identity in Brazil, 1808 to the Present* (Cambridge: Cambridge University Press, 2013) provides an excellent overview. His *Negotiating National Identity: Immigrants, Minorities, and the Struggle for Ethnicity in Brazil* (Durham, NC: Duke University Press, 1999), meanwhile, complicates Brazilian myths about the seamlessness of its multi-ethnic society. Mieko Nishida's *Diaspora and Identity: Japanese Brazilians in Japan and Brazil* (Honolulu: University of Hawai'i Press, 2017) studies closely the unique place of Japanese-Brazilians in two worlds.

The standard work on Brazilian politics and political economy from the Revolution of 1930 to the 1964 military coup is Thomas E. Skidmore's *Politics in Brazil, 1930–1964: An Experiment in Democracy* (New York: Oxford University Press, 2007 [1967]). The Vargas years are very thoroughly covered. A collection of essays by Brazilian scholars tackles the 1930–45 period from a variety of angles: see Luciano Aronne de Abreu and Marco Aurélio Vannucchi, eds., *The Brazilian Revolution of 1930: The Legacy of Getúlio Vargas Revisited* (Eastbourne: Sussex Academic Press,

2021). Another excellent collection of essays on the Vargas years that connects his first and second eras is Jens R. Hentschke, ed., *Vargas and Brazil: New Perspectives* (New York: Palgrave MacMillan, 2006). There are many fine, more narrowly focused studies of this period. Daryle Williams examines how Vargas promoted a unified sense of the nation through patrimony in *Culture Wars in Brazil: The First Vargas Regime, 1930–1945* (Durham, NC: Duke University Press, 2001). Jerry Dávila analyzes education and other policies at this time and connects them to the later part of the Old Republic in *Diploma of Whiteness: Race and Social Policy in Brazil, 1917–1945* (Durham, NC: Duke University Press, 2003). And a classic work on Brazil's increasing ties to the United States at this time is Frank D. McCann's *The Brazilian–American Alliance, 1937–1945* (Princeton: Princeton University Press, 1973).

There is not a well-developed literature in English on the 1945–64 period, but there are a number of good works on a variety of topics. Skidmore's *Politics in Brazil* (see above) remains the best macro-level work on these years. Rafael R. Ioris's *Transforming Brazil: A History of National Development in the Post-War Era* (Hoboken, NJ: Taylor & Francis, 2014) studies the rising consensus on the state's role in economic development. The Brazilian focus on developmentalism and unifying the nation dates to the late nineteenth century and continues into the twenty-first. I study that through the lens of Brazil's embrace of automobility in *Autos and Progress: The Brazilian Search for Modernity* (New York: Oxford University Press, 2010). Sarah Sarzynski's *Revolution in the Terra do Sol: The Cold War in Brazil* (Stanford: Stanford University Press, 2018) analyzes how social movements in the Northeast, especially those seeking land reform, were read by Brazilian and American political leaders as communist and so an existential threat to the status quo in the years leading up to the 1964 military coup.

Maria Helena Moreira Alves's *State and Opposition in Military Brazil* (Austin: University of Texas Press, 1985) remains one of the best works on the start of the coup and the establishment of the authoritarian regime. The single best work on the political economy of this era is Thomas E. Skidmore's *The Politics of Military Rule in Brazil* (New York: Oxford University Press, 1988). The military's unique role in the economy is carefully analyzed by Peter B. Evans in his classic study *Dependent Development: The Alliance of Multinational, State, and Local Capital in* Brazil (Princeton: Princeton University Press, 1979). There is an excellent literature on various forms of resistance to the military regime. Victoria Langland's *Speaking of Flowers: Student Movements and the Making and Remembering of 1968 in Military Brazil* (Durham, NC: Duke University Press, 2013) puts student activism during the dictatorship in historical context by connecting student politics from the Estado Novo through the dictatorship. Christopher Dunn's *Contracultura: Alternative Arts and Social Transformation in Authoritarian Brazil* (Chapel

Hill: University of North Carolina Press, 2016) studies the ways musicians and other artists opposed the dictatorship. James N. Green's *Exile within Exiles: Herbert Daniel, Gay Brazilian Revolutionary* (Durham, NC: Duke University Press, 2018) is a terrific biography of a guerrilla leader who was simultaneously hiding from the regime and keeping his sexuality secret from his comrades in the field. The broader issue of the dictatorship's relationship to sexuality is very well studied in Benjamin A. Cowan's *Securing Sex: Morality and Repression in the Making of Cold War Brazil* (Chapel Hill: University of North Carolina Press, 2016).

The single best source on the military's use of violence against the Brazilian people is the report published by the Archdiocese of São Paulo, *Torture in Brazil: A Shocking Report on the Pervasive Use of Torture by Brazilian Military Governments, 1964–1979* (Austin: University of Texas Press, 1985). The military also used press censorship at this time, as is detailed well by Anne-Marie Smith's *A Forced Agreement: Press Acquiescence to Censorship in Brazil* (Pittsburgh: University of Pittsburgh Press, 1977). The rise of New Labor played an important role in challenging various aspects of this authoritarianism. Margaret Keck details the transition from union organizing to the creation of a powerful political party in *The Workers' Party and Democratization in Brazil* (New Haven: Yale University Press, 1992). The role of new feminist groups in bringing the dictatorship to an end and beginning the process of democratization is analyzed by Sonia E.

Alvarez in *Engendering Democracy in Brazil: Women's Movements in Transition Politics* (Princeton: Princeton University Press, 1990).

The literature on the transition to civilian rule and the establishment of democracy is highly specialized. A very good study of the complex interplay between personalistic politics and party structures is Scott Mainwaring's *Rethinking Party Systems in the Third Wave of Democratization: The Case of Brazil* (Stanford: Stanford University Press, 1999). Fernando Henrique Cardoso provides a firsthand account of these years in *The Accidental President of Brazil: A Memoir* (New York: Public Affairs Press, 2006). Timothy J. Power analyzes conservative politics in this period in *The Political Right in Postauthoritarian Brazil: Elites, Institutions, and Democracy* (University Park: Penn State University Press, 2000).

There is not yet a broad literature in English on the New Republic. There are several terrific works on different aspects of Brazilian society in the post-1985 period. Maureen O'Dougherty's *Consumption Intensified: The Politics of Middle-Class Daily Life in Brazil* (Durham, NC: Duke University Press, 2002) is an excellent snapshot of the middle-class urban experience in the first decade and half of the New Republic. Brian P. Owensby puts Brazil's middle class in historical perspective in *Intimate Ironies: Modernity and the Making of Middle-Class Lives in Brazil* (Stanford: Stanford University Press, 2002). Teresa P.R. Caldeira closely analyzes the dichotomy between the urban poor and middle and upper classes in *City of Walls: Crime, Segregation, and Citizenship in São Paulo* (Berkeley: University of California Press, 2001). Janice Perlman studies the urban poor in dictatorship and democracy in *Favela: Four Decades of Living on the Edge in Rio de Janeiro* (New York: Oxford University Press, 2011).

James Holston details the ongoing political role of popular social movements during the New Republic in *Insurgent Citizenship: Disjunctions of Democracy in Brazil* (Princeton: Princeton University Press, 2009). Wendy Wolford studies closely rural social movements during this period in *The Land is Ours Now: Social Mobilization and the Meaning of Land in Brazil* (Durham, NC: Duke University Press, 2010).

Larry Rohter's *Brazil on the Rise: The Story of a Country Transformed* (New York: Palgrave Macmillan, 2010) provides a positive analysis of the first 25 years of democracy. Dave Zirin presents a much more critical perspective by focusing on Brazil's embrace of mega-events during the 2010s in his *Brazil's Dance with the Devil: The World Cup, the Olympics, and the Fight for Democracy* (Chicago: Haymarket Books, 2016). Roger Kittleson's *The Country of Football: Soccer and the Making of Modern Brazil* (Berkeley: University of California Press, 2014) puts the nation's relationship to the World Cup in an important historical perspective. Jessica Lynn Graham provides another critical analysis of this era by comparing race in politics in the United States and Brazil in *Shifting the Meaning of Democracy: Race, Politics, and Culture in the United States and Brazil* (Berkeley: University of California Press, 2019). And the early years of the Bolsonaro administration are well chronicled in Richard Lapper's *Beef, Bible, and Bullets: Brazil in the Age of Bolsonaro* (Manchester: Manchester University Press, 2021).

Given the prominence of labor in recent Brazilian politics through the Workers' Party and the Lula presidencies, it is worthwhile considering the long history of working people in Brazil. My book *Working Women, Working Men: São Paulo and the Rise of Brazil's Industrial Working Class, 1900–1955* (Durham, NC: Duke University Press, 1993) connects the history of work, popular organizing and protest, industrialists, and the state from the Old Republic through the Vargas years. Molly Ball's *Navigating Life and Work in Old Republic São Paulo* (Gainesville: University of Florida Press, 2020) carefully analyzes women's lives in their factories, neighborhoods, and homes. John D. French has written a terrific biography of Lula's childhood and early years as a trade unionist, although it unfortunately does not study his political campaigns or his presidency. See his *Lula and His Politics of Cunning: From Metalworker to President of Brazil* (Chapel Hill: University of North Carolina Press, 2020).

A seemingly intractable issue for Brazil has been how to combine robust economic growth without continuing to denigrate the environment. A number of excellent works put this tension into historical perspective. The first comprehensive study of the process of environmental destruction in national development is Warren Dean's *With Broadax and Firebrand: The Destruction of the Brazilian Atlantic Forest* (Berkeley: University of California Press, 1997). Several studies focus on the environmental impact of the sugar economy, such as Jennifer Eaglin's *Sweet Fuel: A Political and Environmental History of Brazilian Ethanol* (New York: Oxford University Press, 2022) and Thomas D. Roger's *The Deepest Wounds: An Environmental and Labor History of Sugar in Northeast Brazil* (Chapel Hill: University of North Carolina Press, 2010).

Index

Abertura 106, 108, 109, 142, 180, 190
abolition 4–5, 11, 31, 33–7, 46, 168
　Queiróz Law 35
　Rio Branco Law 35
　Saraiva–Cotegipe Law 35
affirmative action laws, 152, 172, 179
Africa 7, 12, 27, 81, 137, 142, 162
agrarian reform 84, 130
Alckmin, Geraldo 163–4, 187
Aliança Renovadora Nacional, ARENA 91–2, 108, 113
Amazon region 26, 29, 42–3, 59, 97, 112, 120, 160–1, 164, 189
Army, Brazilian military 40–1, 54–5, 60–1, 161–2
　developmentalist policies 48–9, 69
　in politics 36–8, 62, 66, 88
　tenentes 53, 96
Arns, Cardinal Paulo Evaristo 103–4

Bahia 7–8, 25, 40
Banco Nacional de Desenvolvimento Econômico e Social, BNDES 72–3
Belem 42–4
Belo Horizonte 43–4, 78
Belterra 43
Bolsa Família (Family Stipend) 159–60, 162–4, 173, 179
Bolsonaro, Jair 1–4, 181–9, 191, 203
Brasília 1–2, 6, 13, 18, 79, 81, 85, 98, 100, 157, 167, 192

Brazilian Historical and Geographical Institute (Instituto Histórico e Geográfico Brasileiro, IHGB) 10
BRIC countries 16, 165
Brizola, Leonel 113, 117, 126, 145, 146, 169
Bush, George H.W. 127
Bush, George W. 150, 158, 161
Buarque de Holanda, Sérgio 13

Cabral, Pedro Álvarez 6–7, 10
Café Filho, João 76–7
Campos, Roberto 89, 95
Canada 6, 127, 148
Canudos Rebellion 40–1
Capistrano de Abreu, João de 10, 18
Cardoso, Fernando Henrique 140, 141–53, 163, 164, 166, 167–8, 170, 173–5, 179, 187, 190
Carneiro, Enéas 145–6
Castelo Branco, Humberto 88–91, 95
Catholic Church 109, 150
  in politics 37–8, 103–5
Centrão 119, 173–4, 186
Chávez, Hugo 158, 161
Clinton, Bill 148, 150
coffee 24, 26, 27–9, 31, 39, 41–2, 43–7, 49, 51, 60–2, 68, 69, 84, 155, 161
  coffee valorization 47, 55
  National Coffee Council 56
Collor, Lindolfo 54, 127
Collor de Mello, Fernando 126–36, 138–40, 148–9, 175, 192
Companhia Vale do Rio Doce 149, 164
Congress *see* legislature (National Assembly and later Congress)
constitution 21, 76, 84, 88, 92, 135, 136, 188
  1824 23
  1934 53
  1946 66, 71, 81
  1988 63–4, 116–22, 148, 179, 180, 190
  Constitutional Assembly 120–2

Contestado Rebellion 40–1
Costa, Emília Viotti da 13–14
Costa e Silva, Artur 90–1
Covid-19 185, 187, 191
Cuba 80–1
   Cuban Revolution 84

dependency theory 69, 142
DIEESE, Departamento Intersindical de Estaísticas e Estudos Sócio-Econômicos 73, 102, 105, 109
DIP, Departamento de Imprensa e Propaganda 73, 102, 105, 109
Donatary Captaincy 8
Dutra, Eurico Gaspar 63, 66, 70–1, 80

ECLA/CEPAL, Economic Commission for Latin America/Comisión Economica para América Latina 68–70
economic miracle 94, 96, 98–9

Electrobras 83
environmental degradation 29, 100, 160–1, 184
Estado Novo dictatorship 56–7, 61, 65–8, 69–70, 72, 77, 96, 101, 104, 168
eugenics 12, 31, 36, 41, 46
evangelical Christians 156, 182–3

Faoro, Raimundo 13
Farias, Paulo César 134
Figueiredo, João 106, 108, 111
Fonseca, Deodora da 36, 38, 88
Fordlândia 43
Franco, Itamar 131, 135, 137–8, 140, 143, 149
Frente Negra 65, 152
Freyre, Gilberto 11–12, 14–15

Geisel, Ernesto 97–100, 102, 105–6
Germany 28, 154
   West Germany 168

Globo Network (Rede
Globo) 111, 128–30
Goiás 44, 59
Gomes, General Eduardo
63, 71
Goulart, João "Jango" 13,
113, 126, 137–8
Labor Minister 74
president 83, 87–8
vice president 78, 80,
82, 131
Great Britain 21
Grito de Ipiranga 20, 190
Guevara, Ernesto "Ché" 81
Guimarães, Ulysses 120,
126, 133

immigration 11, 31, 35, 37,
43, 46–7, 170
colonos 46–7
impeachment
Dilma Rousseff 16,
178–9
Fernando Collor de Melo
135–6, 139, 149, 175,
184, 191–2
indigenous people 7–9, 12,
45, 60, 161, 184
inflation 73, 83–4, 89–90,
94, 101–2, 106, 112,
115, 122–3, 128,
130–1, 135, 137–40,
141, 143–6, 149, 167,
179
Institutional Acts 87,
91–3, 106
Isabel, Princess 35, 46
Itaipú Dam 18, 97

Kubitschek, Juscelino
77–9, 98, 100, 112,
139, 170, 172

labor 83, 92, 103, 118
labor courts 59, 101
labor laws 55–6, 74
strikes and protests 48,
54–5, 58, 64–7, 73–4,
84, 92, 94, 101–2,
109–10, 114, 154
union tax (*imposto
sindical*) 58, 64
unions 64, 65, 66–7,
72, 104, 109–10, 124,
141
Lacerda, Carlos 75, 88
legislature (National
Assembly and later
Congress) 21, 24, 39,
66, 76, 81, 82, 84,

92, 108, 109, 111, 116–17, 119, 122, 132–3, 134–5, 136, 145, 148, 151, 153, 157, 163, 173–4, 178, 186, 188, 189
Lott, Henrique Teixeira 80
Luís, Washington 49, 51–2
Lula da Silva, Luiz Inácio 2, 4, 16, 122, 124, 153–4, 177–84
  labor leader 118, 141, 154,
  presidential candidate 125–30, 136–7, 141, 145–6, 151, 155–7, 186–92
  president 15, 149, 157–66, 167, 169–70, 172–4, 175, 176, 177

Maluf, Paulo 111, 113, 125
Manaus 42–4
Médici, Emílio Garrastazu 93–4, 96–7, 106
mensalão (Monthly Allowance) 162–3, 165, 174, 175, 180
Mexico 3, 7, 12, 25, 127, 148–9, 150, 155
military *see* Army, Brazilian military
Minas Gerais 9, 25, 26, 39, 43, 49, 51–2, 61, 81, 111, 137, 156, 169, 183
mining 9, 43, 84, 137, 149
Ministry of Labor 53–9, 73–4, 78, 101, 127, 138
Morais e Barros, Prudente José de 39–40
Moro, Sérgio 175, 177, 180–1, 184, 186
Movimento Democrático Brasileiro, MDB 91, 92, 108–9, 137, 180, 187

National Assembly *see* legislature (National Assembly and later Congress)
National Coffee Council (Conselho Nacional do Café or CNC) 56
national myths 3–4, 5, 14
  conciliation 4, 190
  future 4

national myths (*cont.*)
  racial democracy 4–5, 14, 190
Neves, Aécio 175–6, 177–8
Neves, Tancredo 111, 113, 115–16, 119, 137,

Obama, Barack 158
oil/petroleum 16, 72, 99, 106, 164–5, 171–3, 175–7
Operation Car Wash 174–8, 180–2
Order and Progress 13, 69, 139

Package Plan 84
Paraguayan War 32–4, 69, 86
Paraíba Valley 27, 29, 45–6, 61
Paraná 40, 97
Partido Communista do Brasil, PCB (Soviet-aligned) 63, 117, 118, 126
Partido Communista do Brasil, PC do B (Maoist) 117, 118

Partido da Frente Liberal, PFL 111, 115, 117, 118–19, 123, 126, 151, 163
Partido da Social Democracia Brasileira, PSDB 143, 145, 146, 151, 160, 163–4, 170, 176, 187
Partido de Juventude, PJ 126
Partido de Reconstrução Nacional, PRN 126
Partido de Reedificação da Ordem Nacional, PRONA 146
Partido Democrata Cristão, PDC 80
Partido Democrático Social, PDS 108–9, 111, 113, 115, 117, 119, 125
Partido Democrático Trabalhista, PDT 117, 118, 126, 145, 169
Partido do Movimento Democrático Brasileiro, PMDB 109, 111, 113, 115, 116–21, 123, 126, 133, 137, 142–3,

145–6, 148, 157, 170, 178–80
Partido dos Trabalhadores, PT 2, 15, 117–19, 122, 123–5, 129–30, 132, 145–6, 149, 151, 153, 154–8, 162–5, 169–70, 173, 174–9, 180, 183–4, 186–7
Partido Liberal, PL 182, 186
Partido Liberal Social, PLS 182
Partido Popular Socialista, PPS 151
Partido Social Democrático, PSD 62, 63, 71, 77, 80, 143
Partido Social Progressista, PSP 76
Partido Socialista Brasileiro, PSB 187
Partido Trabahista Brasileiro, PTB 62, 66, 71, 76–7, 78, 80, 117–19, 126, 162–3
Partido Trabalhista Nacional, PTN 80
Republican Party 34, 36–7, 36, 52, 63

Paulistas 34, 39, 35, 45–7, 49, 52, 54–5, 133, 140, 156
Pedro I 1, 3, 20–2, 29
Pedro II 22–5, 29, 31–3, 35–8, 46, 87, 88, 117, 139
Peixoto, Floriano 39, 88
Petrobras 72–3, 99, 164, 165, 169, 171, 172, 175, 177
Plano de Integração Nacional, PIN 97
populism 52, 64, 66, 78, 88, 103, 113, 117, 118, 126, 128, 154, 169
Portugal 1, 7, 10, 19–22, 37, 79
Positivism 34
Prado Júnior, Caio 13
Prestes, Júlio 49, 52
Proálcool, National Ethanol Program 18, 99–100, 156

Quadros, Jânio 79–82, 87, 131, 137–8, 143, 145
Quércia, Orestes 145, 146

race/racism 4–5, 11–12, 15, 31, 32, 34, 36, 37–8, 46, 65, 137–8, 142, 152, 173, 179
racial democracy 4–5, 14, 190
Regency 22–4, 87
Rio de Janeiro, city 8, 9, 19, 28, 44, 59, 61, 64, 86
Rio de Janeiro, state 27, 45, 67, 81, 97, 126, 181, 189
Rio Grande do Sul 25, 40, 49, 60, 67, 74, 78, 85, 113, 125–6
Rousseff, Dilma 15, 16, 162, 165, 168, 169–80, 183–4, 190, 191
rubber 24, 26, 28, 42–4, 61
runaway slave communities (*quilombos*) 11, 34, 35, 45, 60

Santa Catarina 40–1
São Paulo, city 2, 42, 44, 48, 53–55, 73, 85, 102, 116, 142, 170, 183
São Paulo, state 20, 25, 27, 28–9, 31, 34, 39, 43, 45–7, 49, 51–2, 54–5, 61, 64, 65, 80, 81, 97, 99, 103, 109–10, 111, 114, 118, 124, 142, 145–6, 153–4, 155–6, 181, 187, 189
 Civil War of 1932 54–5, 59, 156
Sarney, José 111, 115–7, 120–2, 138
Saude, Alimentação, Transportação, Energia, SALTE 70
slavery 1, 3–5, 7, 8–9, 11, 19–20, 22, 26–31, 33–8, 45–6, 60, 61, 93, 142, 151, 168, 189
sugar 8–10, 26–7, 41, 51, 69, 99–100, 155–6
Suplicy, Marta 170

Targets Plan 78–9
Távora, Juarez 77
Telebrás 149

Temer, Michel 170–1, 178–80, 191
Trump, Donald 184

União Democrático Nacional, UDN 63, 68, 71, 74–5, 76–7, 80, 81, 88, 91
United States 4, 6, 11, 14, 28, 33, 36, 60–1, 69, 80, 95, 104, 110, 127, 142, 158, 190, 191

Vargas, Getúlio 49, 52–7, 59–69, 71–80, 83, 88, 92, 94, 98–9, 101–2, 104, 112, 139, 145, 152, 172
Volta Redonda 59–61, 132

Washington Consensus 147–8, 150
Weffort, Francisco 14–5
World Bank 102–3, 138
World Cup 13, 16, 96, 113, 162, 166, 172